80/20 Landlording

Increase Your 80% & Decrease Your 20%

Volume 2

Sheamus P. Clarke

Scott Stellhorn

Published by: (Night Hawk Systems, LLC)

Book Team

Author and Contributor	Sheamus P. Clarke
Author and Contributor	Scott Stellhorn
Editor/Polisher	Nick Hayden
Cover Design & Artwork	Ryan Hoover Sr.

© 2014 by Night Hawk Systems, LLC

All rights reserved. No part of this book may be reproduced, stored in a retrieval system or transmitted in any form or by any means without the prior written permission of the publisher, except by a reviewer who may quote brief passages in a review to be printed in a newspaper, magazine or journal.

First Printing

ISBN: 978-0-9960358-2-8

Published by (Night Hawk Systems, LLC)

1 – Why We Do What We Do 1

2 – The Name Game 6

3 – Proper Tenant Screening 14

4 – A Man and His Cats 22

5 – Handling Tenant Complaints 27

6 – When a Tenant Dies 32

7 – More Important than Rent 37

8 – The Barter System 43

9 – No Answer 48

10 – Reporting to the Credit Bureau 53

11 – Taken to Small Claims Court 55

12 – Smoke 'Em If You Got 'Em 60

13 – Meth Labs: A Rental Owner's Nightmare 66

14 – Contractor Speak 75

15 – Making Carpet Last 80

16 – The Utility Trap 88

17 – How to Lower Property Taxes (Indiana Example) 94

18 – Mower Boy 105

19 – The Bachelor Pad 108

20 – Men in Black 112

Appendix 1 – Indiana Eviction Process 117

Appendix 2 – Eviction Process Ohio 127

Appendix 3 – Michigan Eviction Process 131

Appendix 4 – Ohio Small Claims 143

Appendix 5 – Michigan Small Claims 169

Appendix 6 – Illinois Eviction Process 181

Appendix 7 – Illinois Small Claims Process 186

Acknowledgement

To our wives and families, who allowed us the opportunity to put this book together at the expense of quality time spent with them.

To all those tenants and applicants who have given us both the wisdom and the patience to continue our pursuits as Independent Rental Owners.

Introduction

The response to our initial volume was phenomenal, so we decided to take another crack at helping our readers navigate the world of a landlord. This volume examines how to get the right tenants in the first place using the great tools at www.RealTenantHistory.com as well as how to deal with unique tenant situations. It also tackles some of an Independent Rental Owner's greatest fears and challenges in today's rental culture.

Co-author Sheamus Clarke was working for a privately held company when the executive team underwent significant changes that Sheamus was not happy with and did not want to be a part of. Sheamus looked at what he could do to best secure his and his family's future. He decided to change his employment as well as invest in a rental property.

His new job in software development allowed him to work from home, doing training and support for a small software company. He spent nights and weekends setting up a rental company, reading up on real estate investing, and looking at available properties.

He and his wife purchased a fourplex that had been vacant for some time. Over the next few years, they acquired more properties and now manage and maintain 25 properties.

Scott Stellhorn's in-laws were landlords in the 1980s and introduced him to the concept of rental income. His father-in-law did 95% of the repairs on the units, from plumbing to electrical to roofing. Scott gained his training in maintenance from him, which saved him tremendous money in the future.

While in college, Scott purchased his first fixer-upper to rent and sold it the first year to the tenants who occupied the home.

He graduated college in 1983 with an Associate's Degree in computer science and started his computer technology career writing COBOL for a distribution company in Fort Wayne.

While working full-time, he increased his holdings on fixer-upper multi-unit buildings and, in turn, increased his rental income. As you will read in the upcoming chapters, there were times of joy mixed with "What am I doing?" In the end, the benefits of being an Independent Rental Owner outweighed the issues he encountered.

Forward

Between the two of us, there is more than 45 years of combined landlord experience. From this comes endless lessons and stories.

What you will find in this book is a compilation of the trials and tribulations we have experienced—the extraordinary work required in evictions, small claims, maintenance, property management, and people skills.

You might think this book is simply about terrible tenant experiences. Believe us, we could have written that book. But for every really bad tenant we've had, we've had even more great tenants. Some tenants have become friends. We've invited them to our homes, celebrated birthdays and holidays with them.

There is also a lot of work that has nothing to do with the properties themselves, issues arising from laws, regulations, and local ordinances. In this volume, we've included topics like property taxes, credit bureaus, and utilities, as well as appendices on eviction and small claims procedures in various states.

But why call this book 80/20 Landlording?

It's rooted in something known as the Pareto principle, which states that in many cases, roughly 80% of the effects come from 20% of the causes.

Business-management consultant Joseph M. Juran suggested the principle and named it after Italian economist Vilfredo Pareto, who observed in 1906 that 80% of the land in Italy was owned by 20% of the population; Pareto also observed that 20% of the pea pods in his garden contained 80% of the peas.

It's become a common rule of thumb in business. For example, someone might say, "Eighty percent of your sales come from 20% of your clients."

It's not hard to find other applications for entrepreneurs and business managers:

- Eighty percent of a company's profits come from 20% of its customers.
- Eighty percent of a company's complaints come from 20% of its customers.
- Eighty percent of a company's profits come from 20% of the time its staff spends.
- Eighty percent of a company's sales come from 20% of its products.
- Eighty percent of a company's sales are made by 20% of its sales staff.

Knowing this, many businesses can improve profitability by focusing on the most effective areas and by eliminating, ignoring, automating, delegating, or retraining the rest, as appropriate.

These ideas are transferable to the Independent Rental Owner.

For instance, it's useful to remember that during a normal day, only 20% of your activity really matters—the most important 20% of your efforts produces 80% of your results. Identify and focus on those things in your 20%. Remind yourself of this vital 20% when the fire drills of everyday life happen. If something in the schedule has to slip, if something isn't going to get done, make sure it's not part of that 20%.

Another truth from the landlord business is this: Twenty percent of your tenants will cause 80% of your headaches.

This book is written so that you can focus more on the 20% of your work that matters and less on the 20% of the tenants and regulations that cause all the headaches.

We've learned a lot over our 45 combined years. We've found tricks and tools that work. We'll refer to one again and again— Real Tenant History (www.realtenanthistory.com). But there are plenty of others, from legal processes to hard-won knowledge. It's all here to aid you, whatever might come.

Being a landlord is not easy, but it *is* rewarding. We hope our experiences, written by landlords, for landlords, can make your work that much easier and that much more rewarding.

Sheamus P. Clarke

Scott Stellhorn

1 – Why We Do What We Do

We at Real Tenant History have been holding Library Workshops in Indiana, Michigan, and Ohio since the release of Volume 1 in early 2014. You can check out our Facebook page (facebook.com/realtenanthistory) to see our schedule or you can visit the Events Calendar at realtenanthistory.com.

These workshops have once again demonstrated the quality and conviction of those who own rental properties.

In almost every case, the Independent Rental Owners (IROs) I speak to never looked at the rental business as a way to get rich quick. They all have the best motivations behind the purchase of their rental properties, just as I did when I bought my first property.

My wife and I got into the business for every reason except to get rich quick. The first property we bought was a vacant, rundown place that at one time had five units, two upstairs with three downstairs, with no off-street parking.

The previous owner had no interest in renovating and was even renting out one of the units while two others were fire damaged. The rented unit's roof leaked, but the owner had no intention of fixing it. We saw the property sitting as an eyesore in the middle of beautiful single-family homes. We decided to go to the court house to find out who owned the property. We then called the owner and asked if we could meet him and check out the property. He agreed. Within two weeks, we were the new owners.

Sale price of the property, as is—$24,000.

The property was over 100 years old. It had a small basement the tenants did not have regular access to, except in case of storms. The first floor was just over 2,300 square feet. The upstairs was about 1,700 square feet. The stairs attached to the north and south side of the property, by which you reached the second floor, were pulling off. There was no carpet anywhere, only wood floor—and not nice wood floor.

Now the work began.

My wife and I spent nine months renovating, tackling projects in the following order:

- Making the property weather tight.
- Adding new 110 Amp service to all units.
- Adding new heating and cooling.
- Adding new subfloors.
- Installing all-new drywall.
- Installing new kitchens and baths.
- Appling new paint.
- Installing all-new carpet and flooring.

And $65,000 later, with 90% of the labor provided by me and my wife, we were ready to rent the units.

We held an open house for the neighbors and community so that everyone could see the work we had done to make the property worthy of the neighborhood. We even received a plaque from the city for renovating a rundown property.

We still own the property today. With continued maintenance, it stays in good condition and still fits well in the neighborhood.

My story is only one of many examples of why people get into the rental business. When I meet fellow IROs at workshops, I encounter similar values and beliefs. They did not expect to get rich. Though they all purchase property for various reasons, they understand that over time they will build equity in the property and provide quality housing to tenants who need it.

I've heard a variety of specific reasons for embarking on the life of an IRO. Some of these include:

- Wanting to purchase a property they previously lived in.
- Wanting to make sure the property did not end up in the wrong hands.
- Purchasing a property next to them to keep out bad tenants.
- Wanting to create a retirement vehicle.

The reasons go on and on.

It's a gross mischaracterization to think a landlord is rolling in the dough. In most cases, a landlord's life consists of renting units, cleaning and repairing units, and managing tenants. A landlord works hard to ensure his rentals are in good condition.

Of course, *some* landlords are in it for the money, but in most cases you'll find a stark difference. Their rental units have lots of undone maintenance; they have a high tenant turnover rate; and their vacancy rate is high.

This is wrong.

When a landlord rents to an individual, they create a partnership. The landlord has certain responsibilities, and the tenant has others. In a healthy partnership, both parties hold each other accountable for those respective responsibilities. Neither party should take advantage of the other.

On September 18, 2014, I had an interesting discussion with one of the workshop participants. Phil has six rental properties, each one a single-family home. All are on the same street, side by side.

"How's the quality of the tenants?" I asked him. "How long do they stay, on average?"

"Well, my shortest tenancy was seven years. The longest was 13."

These are astounding numbers. Typical tenancy rates are between one and two years.

With more questioning, I discovered Phil's secret. His rents are extremely low, about 35% below the going rate for his area. He's renting a one-bedroom, single-family house with a nice yard and basement for $350 a month. The area's average is $490 a month.

It's the same thing with his two-bedroom homes. He's renting those for an average of $450 when the going rate is closer to $630.

No wonder his tenants stay so long.

Phil's one of those IROs who rents properties as a retirement vehicle. He knows his rents are low and he uses it as a way to retain great tenants. This makes sense—to a point.

"Have you ever considered raising your rent?" I asked.

"No. I don't want a good tenant to move because I raise the rent."

This is why it's important to know the going rates in your community. I showed Phil that he was missing out on about $12,500 a year due to his low rent. "But even if you raise your rent, you're still below or even with the going rate. I don't think your good tenants will leave. If you provide good housing, it's worth the money to them."

Phil considered the numbers and my reasoning. "I may have to rethink my strategy."

If he does, it's not about getting rich. It's about the partnership between tenant and landlord. A get-rich landlord doesn't take care of his tenants. But a good landlord deserves a fair return on his labor.

This volume is designed to make you a better landlord so that you can provide quality housing to your tenants. In return, you'll get and keep the kind of tenants every landlord wants.

2 – The Name Game

In September 2013, I had a single mother move into a two-bedroom apartment with her infant son. She was working as an assistant manager at Taco Bell, so income was not an issue. Her personal references checked out.

The only problem was she had never leased an apartment in her name, so there was no way to check with her past landlords about their experiences.

Or so I thought.

On her application she put Elizabeth L. Handshoe (name changed), and this name is what I used for my background checks.

The rent was on time for the first six months, October through March.

April came, and I received a call from Elizabeth. "I quit my job and got a new one," she told me. "I'm going to move closer to my mom so she can help with child care. My new job isn't as flexible with hours."

"As long as the apartment is in the same condition you found it in when you leave, that should be fine. I'll be able to rent it out pretty easily. I'll waive the balance of your lease, too."

"That'll be great. Thanks for understanding. I'll get April's rent out right away." And she did.

Later that week, I received a phone call from a realtor in the city where her mother lived. "Could you give me a reference for Beth Handshoe? She's currently living in your apartment."

I told him Elizabeth was terminating her lease early to move in with her mother, and as long as everything was in good order when she left, I wouldn't charge her any additional rent or fees.

May was approaching, so I texted her to make sure we were still on schedule for her to vacate the premises by May 1. "Yes, that's still good," she told me.

May arrived. I stopped by the apartment and looked in a window. A lot of her belongings were still there, so I decided to call. No answer. I texted her. No reply. I figured she was working. I gave her a couple days to respond.

On May 4, I texted again. It was Sunday, so I thought I'd get a response. And I did.

"I have moved everything out and cleaned."

Since she had moved out, I was now able to check the unit. I discovered that what she meant to say was not I have moved everything out and cleaned," but "I have moved everything *that I wanted, and I did not have time to clean.*"

Mail was spread on the floor, including these fine-looking bills:

- Water – three months past due - $147.50
- Electric – three months past due - $918.08
- Cable – never paid in full - $332.14
- Medical – multiple bills in collections - $2000+

The most interesting thing, though, was not the number of outstanding bills, but the names on the bills.

- My lease – Elizabeth L. Handshoe
- Realtor – Beth Handshoe
- Cable company – Elizabeth Handshoe
- Electric company – Beth L Handshoe
- Water company – Linda E Handshoe

- Medical collections – Beth Hanshoe

No wonder I had found no past rental experience on her!

At Real Tenant History, we use a proprietary "nickname" database during searches to look up all variations of a name for our customers.

Well, name games aside, I still had move-out pictures to take. Here they are:

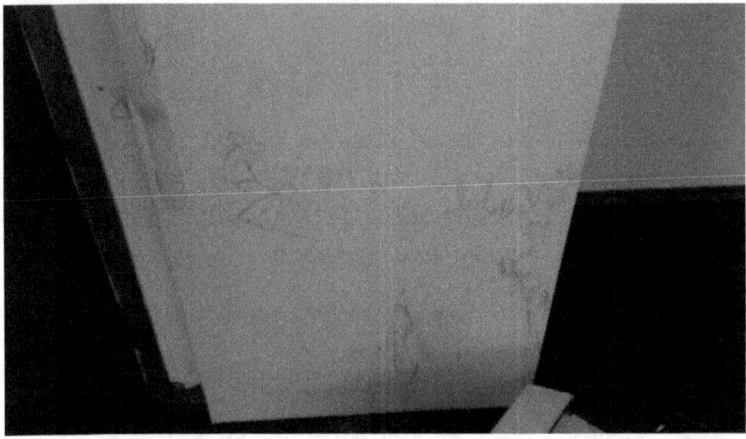

Here's a fridge with Sharpie Marker all over it. It must have made a great memo pad.

Spaghetti, anyone? It looks like she dumped the whole box on the floor—for some reason.

Fingernail polish! Considering the height, this is probably the child's doing.

The always entertaining inside-of-the-fridge pic.

Can you see all the stuff/dirt on the counter? One sweep of a rag would have made all the difference.

Peeled laminate on the interior doors, always a welcome sight.

Nope, nothing left behind. Nothing to see here. Move on.

Quest to destroy blinds—complete.

Obviously, I was annoyed that Beth, or Lizzy, or the tenant formerly known as Elizabeth L. Handshoe, had left the apartment in such terrible condition. I decided that since she had not kept her side of the deal I would charge her for the entire lease amount.

See the Security Deposit Notice to Tenant – Termination of Tenancy Report on the next page for how this looked.

Once we do go to small claims, I know I cannot charge her for months in which I have a new tenant in the unit, but I can explain that to the courts at that time.

The lesson here is that when you search a tenant's history, make sure you check all available aliases so you don't miss important information like I did. And if you search at realtenanthistory.com, the site does all the hard work for you.

Security Deposit Notice to Tenant - Termination of Tenancy

Forwarding Address:

[redacted] Kendallville, IN 46755	Attainment, Inc. P.O. Box 563 Kendallville, IN 46755 [redacted]

Sent May 27th, 2014

You must respond to this notice by mail within 7 days after receipt of same, otherwise you will forfeit the amount claimed for damages.

On or about _ May 20th, 2014_____, your occupancy of the premises commomly known as _[redacted]_____, Kendallville, IN 46755 terminated pursuant to statute, this notice is given to advise you of the items charged against your security deposit as follows:

(A)	Rent Deposit		$475.00
(B)	Pet Deposit $_____ Less $_____ (Non Refundable)		
(C)	Key Deposit		$0
(D)	Net Deposit Refundable		($475.00)

Tenant Moved without notifying Landlord after 7 days

CHARGES AGAINST SECURITY DEPOSIT — Cost to Repair/Replace

1. Paint Walls (18.0 Hours) — $ 564.00
2. Remove Items left behind (4 Cubic Yards) — $ 210.00
3. Clean Fridge/Stove/Kitchen Sink/Sweep Floors/Clean Entire Bathroom — $ 305.00
4. Replace Blinds (4 Damaged @ $25.00) + Slider Door Blind — $ 172.00
5. Carpet Cleaning ($234.30 + 50.00) — $ 284.30
6. Remove Nail Polish from Cupboards (3 Hours) — $ 75.00
7. Replace Locks, Keys never returned — $ 60.00
8. Removal of Sharpie Marker written on Fridge (3 Hours) — $ 125.00
9.

(E)	Total Damages		$1,795.30
(F)	Unpaid Rent	Moved Out Early May, June, July, Aug, Sept 2014	$ 2,375.00
(G)	Other Charges		
		Court Charges $0.00	
		Late Fees $ 375.00	
		Attorney Fees: _____ * Attorney Fees at 40% of Claim	
		Other $____ Explain _____	$375.00
(H)	Total Charges against security deposit	(E) plus (F) plus (G)	$4,545.30
(I)	Refund of Rent From _____ to _____ @ $____ per day		$0.00
	BALANCE	(D) minus (H) Plus (I)	($4,070.30)

If Positive Balance Due You *** Check Enclosed ***
If Negative-Amount Due us *** **Please pay within 7 days** *** If Payment not re[cut off] Matter will be turned over to our Attorney.

Remit Payment to :   **Attainment, Inc.**
P.O. Box 563
Kendallville, IN 46755
(260) 347-5835

Date: _____   Signed by: _____

3 – Proper Tenant Screening

Screening tenants is vital. You've probably heard the horror stories or have been personally involved in one. A drug conviction that shows up on an applicant's background check. The would-be tenant who's listed in a sexual predator registry. Those apparently conscientious tenants who, you come to find out, trashed their last apartment and blamed their landlord for the damage.

And there's always an excuse to explain away these facts.

In our forty-plus years of rental experience, we've heard every excuse imaginable.

Face it. Today's culture makes it imperative to screen prospective tenants *thoroughly*.

If nothing else, proper screening helps you avoid costly cleanup and repair. Consider what kind of time and money it takes to restore a rental unit after the tenants use it as a meth lab! (See Chapter 12.) That's no longer a hypothetical situation. If you're like most Independent Rental Owners (IRO), you simply don't have the funds and resources for that kind of cleanup.

Of course, costly cleanup isn't all you have to worry about.

The photos above document what tenants did to their rental unit in just 42 days! This apartment was in excellent condition when they moved in. After their eviction, it took more than $2,500 to return the property to its original state.

The landlord reported, "The process used to screen these tenants included a credit report, a background check, and a call to two personal references. But we did not vet these tenants using www.RealTenantHistory.com. If we had, we would have discovered they had done the same thing to two prior landlords. We could have saved ourselves a great deal of grief."

Conventional tenant screening leaves you vulnerable to Tenant Predators®.

Tenant Predators® is our term for tenants who have a history of bad behavior. Besides being capable of trashing a unit as illustrated above, there are also tenants who

- were evicted from a previous apartment for possession of illegal drugs.
- had landlords kick them out for failing to pay their rent on time.
- ignored repeated landlord warnings about not keeping pets on the property.
- ran illicit businesses out of their rental unit.

- disturbed the peace numerous times, aggravating neighbors with loud stereos and TVs, violent domestic arguments, rowdy parties, or other shenanigans.

Whatever the reason, you're not going to hear the truth from the tenant in question. No, you're going to have to dig for it. But the basic digging tools—credit reports, background checks, personal references, employment verifications—while helpful, often miss the kind of vital information you need to make a sound rental decision.

What you really need are tenant reviews from a prospect's previous landlords.

That's one of the primary benefits of Real Tenant History—access to other landlords' experience with your potential tenant.

Portrait of a Real Tenant Predator®

Let's take an example of a real Tenant Predator® and the havoc she left in her wake.

We won't use her name. We'd like to show her a kindness she never showed us or any of her previous landlords.

Over the course of 21 years, this woman twice filed for bankruptcy to clear her debts. This ended up costing her prior landlords more than $21,000 in lost rent and unpaid repairs and damages.

Her history includes eight different property managers or landlords with a combined 11 issues with her during this time. She also had 41 civil, criminal, or citation cases filed against her that made it to some local or state court. That's two cases every year!

Of the 29 civil cases, seven went unserved, so the $21,000 cited above isn't even the full extent of the damage she caused.

A single housing community had four separate bad experiences with her: a small claims filing in 1992 (unserved), another small claims filing in 1996 for $595, which entailed no judgment, a 2011 eviction (unserved), and finally, a served 2011 eviction.

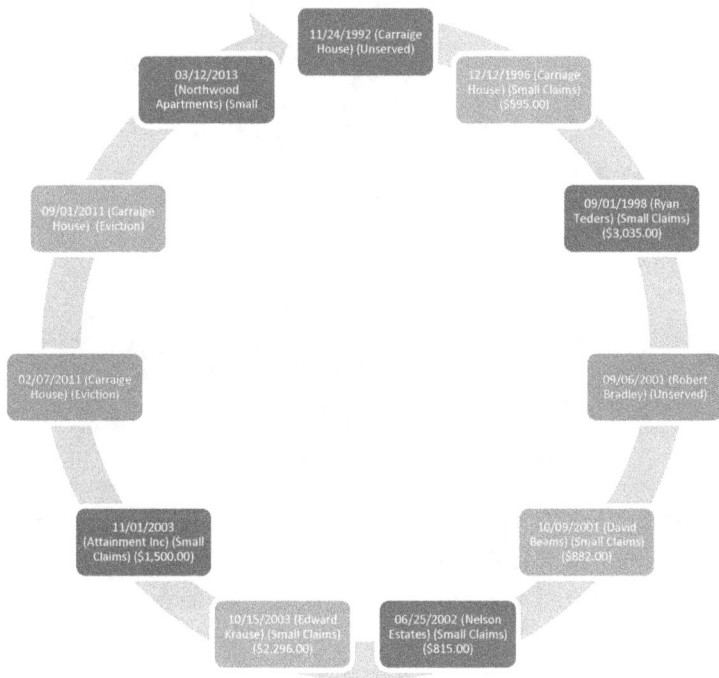

This community kept good records of this woman's behavior. Why, then, did it continue to rent to her? Good question, and one we can't answer. The cycle of her behavior was predictable. She's the perfect definition of a Tenant Predator. Like most such predators, she doesn't care about receiving judgments against her. She can just file bankruptcy every ten years and be done with them!

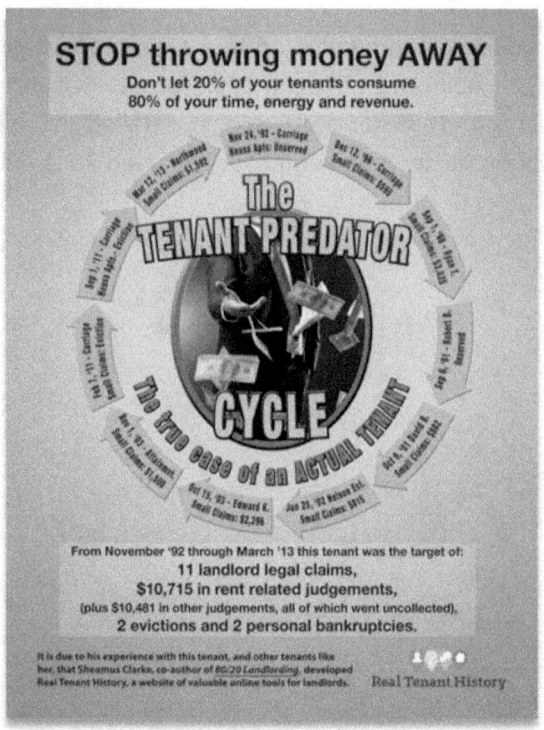

Had Real Tenant History been available after the first few incidents of this woman's irresponsibility, future landlords would have known her M.O. and refused to rent to her.

What makes Real Tenant History® your best screening option?

Real Tenant History was created *by* landlords *for* landlords. Who, after all, knows better the joys, the sorrows, and the myriad details attendant to owning and operating rental properties?

With Real Tenant History you get a complete toolbox to assist you in managing your properties with greater efficiency and effectiveness. That includes the most comprehensive tools yet available for screening tenants.

When you rent to someone who becomes a good tenant, you're justified in feeling you screened that tenant well. But just the opposite happens when you rent to a Tenant Predator®.

That's where Real Tenant History helps you, as no other IRO program does. It helps you avoid the guilt, the hassle, and the heartache that renting to a Tenant Predator® brings.

Real Tenant History gives you choices in the kind of screening data you record. You create tenant profiles that convey the information you find important, including reviews of your current and past tenants. The program also lets you record tenant reviews from other landlords.

Now when a new prospect applies for a rental, a previous landlord's review of that prospect is weighed against the criteria you've chosen. The entire tenant review and rating process is geared uniquely to your requirements.

Here's what a typical IRO-individualized Real Tenant History profile looks like:

Real Tenant History Dashboard:

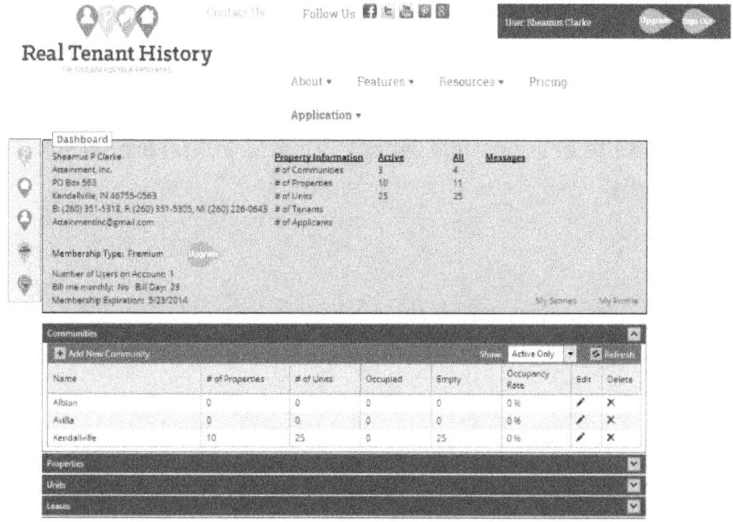

Real Tenant History Customer profile Weights:

There's a lot more to Real Tenant History than we've mentioned here, but proper tenant screening is a vital part of your business success—and your peace of mind! Don't suffer through more excuses and lies. By using Real Tenant History's tenant screening, you have the best possible assurance that you've selected the best possible tenants for your rental properties.

4 – A Man and His Cats

In May 2014, I received a call from "Tom," a prospective tenant. His first question after I told him about the available unit was, "Do you allow pets?"

This is usually a dead giveaway that the tenant owns some sort of pet that other Independent Rental Owners will not accept.

"What kind of pet?" I asked.

"Cats."

"Cats," is very different than "a cat." I asked him how many he meant.

"I have three cats."

The unit I was offering was a small one-bedroom apartment on the first floor of a duplex.

I asked my usual questions:

- Have they been spayed or neutered?
- Have they been declawed?
- Have they been litter box trained?

After answering, he told me, "The cats are service animals."

My first thought was, "Really? Cats?"

"I have documentation," he continued. "I'd be happy to bring it with me when I come to look at the apartment."

I set up an appointment for him to look over the apartment. Since I had a couple days before he came, I decided to do some research on service animals.

According to Wikipedia, the definition of a service animal is as follows:

"Service animals are animals that have been trained to perform tasks that assist people with disabilities."

It continues to say that dogs are the most common service animals, though monkeys, birds, and horses can also be used. Legally, only dogs and, in certain conditions, miniature horses are service animals in the United States.

According to the Americans with Disabilities Act (ADA), a dog is considered a "service dog" if it has been "individually trained to do work or perform tasks for the benefit of a person with a disability." These tasks include walking, seeing, speaking, breathing, working, etc.

Typical documentation for a service animal resemble the pictures below:

After a bit more search, I found a document with the subject "Service Animals and Assistance Animals for People with Disabilities in Housing and HUD-Funded Programs" detailing how service animals relate to the United States Fair Housing Act (http://portal.hud.gov/).

While legally only dogs are considered service animals, and service animal excludes emotional support animals, the document states that "Persons with disabilities may request a reasonable accommodation for any assistance animal, including an emotional support animal, under both the FHAct and Section 504."

Further research showed that while service animals were originally trained to assist those with visual impairments, they have also been trained to help with "post-traumatic stress disorder, bipolar disorder, panic disorder and other mental illnesses, autism, intellectual disabilities, epilepsy, diabetes, hearing impairments and other physical disabilities." (http://www.bazelon.org/Where-We-Stand/Community-Integration/Psychiatric-Service-Animals-and-Civil-Rights.aspx).

The use of these emotional support animals can help calm their owners and alleviate many of the symptoms associated with mental and emotional stress.

One of the most interesting things I found was that almost any kind of animal can be considered an emotional support animal.

All this research showed me that the definition of service animal was wider than I had originally thought, but I still didn't know what I needed to. Were Tom's three cats really service animals? In any case, I was looking forward to meeting Tom and seeing what type of documentation he had to show me.

When Tom arrived, I found he drove one of those motorized "get-around" scooters since he was overweight and had other medical conditions that made it difficult for him to get around easily.

After I showed Tom the apartment, he said he was interested in renting and completed a rental application.

Tom also showed me his documentation, a letter from the Health Department showing that his cats were service animals. It didn't say *how* they were service animals, but I assumed they were for emotional support.

"I've had trouble in the past with renting because of pets," he told me after presenting his documentation. Apparently, one time a landlord became quite abusive toward Tom and his pets, and the ADA fined the landlord $400 after a hearing.

I could have come up with reasons not to rent to Tom, too, but after talking to him I discovered he had been renting from another landlord for more than eight years and had never missed a payment. (I verified this using realtenanthistory.com.) He had always been prompt with his payments, as well.

His current landlord had become ill and managing the apartments had become too much work for him. He was letting them go back to the bank.

Tom's cats did not seem to be a problem based on my policy or my screening, and they were obviously helpful to him, so I leased the unit to him and his three cats.

The moral of the story is to do your research whenever you encounter a new issue. Just because a situation is unusual doesn't mean it should automatically count against a potential tenant. There are a number of valuable tools at www.realtenanthistory.com to assist landlords with these types of questions.

5 – Handling Tenant Complaints

Can't we all just get along?

Nobody but a true masochist *enjoys* confrontation. But disagreements can arise even between good friends. Sometimes, these disagreements can get tense.

Business relationships, like that between a landlord and his tenant, are especially ripe for conflict. How you handle these conflicts says a lot about you, not just about your landlording skills, but about your character. As a landlord or property owner, you have a responsibility to yourself and to your business to keep tenant complaints from escalating out of hand. They must be handled wisely and with a level head.

From 'in your face!' ...

If you have any experience as a landlord or property owner, you know that tenants can complain about...well, pretty much anything: neighbors, parking arrangements, repairs (both major and minor), utilities, rent increases, you name it! Before delving into how to handle tenant complaints, here are two points of caution:

- **Every Situation Is Unique:** Every person has a different personality and different triggers. This makes it hard to know how a certain person will react in a conflict. Observe the other person carefully to determine the best way to approach someone who may react badly to the current conflict.

- **Be Safe:** If you think your safety could be in jeopardy, remove yourself from the situation. Always have someone else with you when confronting a potentially difficult person. If the situation looks as if it might become violent, leave immediately and contact the proper authorities. Do not put your career or life in peril over a tenant's complaint!

... to a handshake!

Each type of complaint, and each person complaining, has to be handled in its own way. How you adjust your response depends largely on your intuition. However, there are certain tactics you can use in every case to increase your chances of success. Remember, how *you* respond to the conflict can have a huge impact on the outcome. You can't control the other person's response, but you can control yours.

Be an "Active" Listener

Actually listen to what the tenant is telling you.

For example, say you're aware of a small basement leak that reveals itself whenever there's a heavy rain. If the tenant calls to tell you about the leak, don't dismiss it simply because it's already on your radar. In fact, the tenant may be telling you about *another* leak, this one from a burst pipe that needs immediate repair.

By not listening carefully and asking questions, like the exact location of the leak and the strength of the water flow, you could wind up not only with an unhappy tenant but with a hefty repair bill as well.

Be Available

If a tenant feels you're never available, he'll grow frustrated more quickly.

Establish normal business hours when a tenant can contact you. For instance, from 9 a.m. to 6 p.m. on weekdays. During these hours, respond to tenant phone calls and emails without delay.

Let the tenant know, as well, that he should not contact you outside these hours except in an emergency—and make sure you and the tenants are on the same page regarding what constitutes an emergency.

Many tenants will phone you about a problem. They may even leave a note on your doorstep or with your office receptionist. But nowadays, tenants are even more likely to communicate in one of the following ways:

- **Texting.** If you aren't currently set up for text messaging, you're missing out on a simple and cost-effective tool for communicating with your tenants.

- **Email.** Nearly everyone has an email, and it's a great way for tenants to communicate with their landlords. Email gives you a written copy, with a time stamp, of a tenant's complaints, as well as a quick and easy way to reply.

- **Social Media.** One of the worst things a landlord or property manager can be is uninformed. To be informed these days, you need an account with Facebook, Twitter, LinkedIn, and other social media. If a tenant doesn't feel you're dealing with an issue properly, he'll likely use social media to vent. Right or wrong, true or false, tenants can quickly spread all kinds of rumors and innuendo about you online. You need to be aware of what's being said. Social media keeps you in the loop. You can communicate directly with tenants on the sites they spend time on, and you can better maintain control of your brand image.

Show Genuine Concern.

Dismissing a tenant's complaint is a sure way to create hostility. It doesn't matter how much validity you give privately to the complaint, you still need to make the tenant feel it's important to you and that you'll do everything in your power to address it as soon as possible.

You want tenants to know you're on their side. Unless, of course, you prefer being their "Evil Landlord." In that case, be prepared to go out of business soon!

Address Complaints in a Timely Manner

By timely, we mean anywhere from a few minutes to a few hours, depending on the form of communication. It also depends on the severity of the complaint.

We're not talking about how quickly you resolve the issue at the heart of the complaint. What most clients are initially looking for is an acknowledgement from you that you've listened to their complaint and that there is a timetable for when you plan to address it.

This timetable depends on the issue. A gas leak or broken front door lock needs to be taken care of immediately. A broken kitchen cabinet or cracked tile can wait a day or two. What's most important is that you are honest with your tenants about what you can do and how quickly you can do it.

A simple text message, email, or phone call indicating you've received the complaint can go a long way toward smoothing landlord-tenant relations.

Be Professional

Above all, conduct yourself in a professional manner.

This is your business. You cannot allow emotions to cloud your judgment. If a tenant is screaming, do not scream back. Do not curse. Do not put yourself in legal jeopardy by threatening or by using tactics such as ignoring maintenance requests or fiddling with a tenant's utilities.

It's your responsibility to stay cool and levelheaded at all times. If you do, tenant complaints will never get the better of you. Instead, you'll find your tenant relationships more pleasant, your business stronger...and you future brighter!

6 – When a Tenant Dies

In January 2004, I experienced my first tenant death.

Tenant #1:

He was an older gentleman, probably in his late 60's. He had no brother or sister, and his parents were deceased. A friend would check on him every couple days, and it was during one such visit that she discovered he had passed away.

The friend called the police, who called the coroner. The body was removed. She then called me to let me know what had happened.

I wasn't sure what I was supposed to do, but I did change the locks.

Over the next few days, three different people called, wanting to go through the man's belongings. I called the police to see if they knew who the executor of the estate was, but they didn't know.

So I went to my attorney to figure out my options. Since I live in a small town, the attorney was able to find that the man had a will and that the friend was being assigned as executor of the estate.

I told this to the people who called and the calls stopped.

I met with the executor at the apartment about five days after the gentleman's passing. Together, we entered the apartment. The friend found the gentleman's checkbook, which was nearly empty, and a few unpaid bills.

"I'm done," she told me. She left and I never saw her again. I was left with an apartment full of a dead man's belongings. After five days of sitting empty, there was now a strong odor.

I began a careful inspection. What I found was rather disgusting.

I opened the fridge. Inside were a hotdog and a cola. There was no other food in the apartment.

In the medicine chest was enough cold medicine to alleviate the coughs and stuffed noses of a small village. Viagra pills were scattered throughout the apartment.

Towels were laid on nearly every sitting surface. When I moved them, it looked as if the tenant had lost control of his bodily functions several weeks prior to passing away.

There was a computer as well as more than 25 boxes of pornographic pictures printed from the Internet. There was another 500 VHS tapes full of the same stuff.

I asked a friend of mine if he would help me remove the contents from the apartment. He agreed, and we spent 12 hours on a Saturday hauling everything to a local transfer site.

Then I repainted, cleaned, and had the carpet cleaned. I was out $1500, but the unit was ready to rent again!

Basic Guidelines

I have had three tenants die in my 20 years of rental experience, and the steps I took to regain possession of the rental unit was different in each case.

The first thing to understand is that a lease does not end with the death of the tenant. It continues until the lease's expiration date unless legal action is taken to terminate it and regain possession.

As in the case above, the lease naturally passes to the estate of the deceased tenant just as personal property does. The estate is then liable for rental payments. The executor, however, cannot simply pass the lease into a new person's name without the landlord's consent. If the landlord refuses to consent to an assignment of the lease in a way the court finds unreasonable, the court can terminate the lease.

A landlord can also take legal action to terminate the lease in accordance with state and local law.

No matter the case, after the death of a tenant the landlord must determine who the lease now properly refers to and not let friends or family members take actions with the past tenant's property or unit. The landlord should work only with the executor of the estate.

Tenant #2:

The second tenant who died was actually renting the same apartment as the first, three years later. He was a great tenant and a nice guy. He was friendly with the neighbors and even referred some of his friends from church to my units.

The lady who moved into the apartment next to his checked on him daily to see if he needed anything.

One day, she found him sitting in his chair, but when she called his name, he did not respond. He had had a heart attack earlier that day.

This tenant did have family close by. Within a week, they had moved all his belongings. They cleaned the apartment and even had the carpets cleaned. Since the rent was paid through the end of the month and they did such a great job with the cleaning, I returned his full deposit to his daughter.

Tenant # 3:

And now for something completely different….

The third tenant lived in a four-bedroom house. He was single, but he had two daughters from a previous marriage.

He and a buddy had originally rented the house, but the buddy had moved out several years prior to his death. He, his two daughters, and one grandchild lived in the house.

One day I called the house about that month's rent being late. That's when I discovered their father had passed away—*three weeks before.*

"We're clearing things out. We'll let you know when we're done."

One week went by. Then two weeks. Then three. It was nearly the end of the month. I hadn't received rent for the month or heard anything from the daughters. I decided to stop by to check on the status of the cleaning.

One of the daughters met me at the door. "It's taking longer than we thought. I think we'll be done in another week or so."

"That'll be fine."

I didn't hear anything from them that week, either, so I returned to the house. No one answered the door. I let myself in. Lo and behold! What a mess! They had vacated the premises—but nothing had been cleaned or moved out.

They had played on my sympathy and been squatting for weeks.

I opened some mail. I discovered that they had run up their father's cell bill to more than $2,000 and had maxed out two credit cards, totaling more than $10,000.

I knew this because the purchases had been made after their father had died. Since I knew the daughters' names, I called the credit card companies and informed them of the tenant's date of death and who had access to the credit cards after his death. I don't know what happened with this, but I hope the credit card companies went after the daughters.

It took me more than a week to clear out his belongings. After that, it was normal cleaning, painting, and carpet-cleaning.

I was out $1,200 in rent, plus $700 in cleaning.

In hindsight, I should have changed the locks as soon as I found out he had passed away.

7 – More Important than Rent

Everyone has that tenant: "I'm sorry, but my rent will be late this month because…." The *because* changes month to month, but the rent is always late, without fail.

Oh, they pay. That's good. You're getting your rent. But it's late. Always.

I've had a *lot* of these tenants over the years. I never cease to be amazed at how they prioritize their rent payment.

One illustration of the way these tenants prioritize badly happened to me recently. This tenant finally *did* fail to pay rent, but the issues involved are the same.

This tenant called to tell me the rent would be late because he had just spent the money paying the electric bill.

Now, the next week I received a notice that the electricity would be turned off the next day if the bill was not paid immediately. Conclusion—the tenant had not, in fact, paid the bill.

The electricity got shut off. After that, I never saw the tenant again.

Proper procedure required I hang a "10-Day Notice to Quit" on the door and wait 10 days. Sunday evening, I posted the notice.

Monday: No sign of the tenant.

Tuesday: I received a text from the tenant indicating he would be by to pay the rent. (This never happened.)

Wednesday: Nothing.

Thursday: Nothing.

Friday: I noticed a truck parked outside the apartment, furniture in the bed.

Saturday: The truck was back.

I haven't stopped by to talk to the tenant. Since I'd already notified him of my intentions, stopping by the rental unit could only cause additional issues.

Sunday: Nothing.

Monday: The tenant called to say he had moved everything out and cleaned the apartment. "Can I get my deposit?" he asked. "I'll have to check out the unit first," I replied.

Monday: Nothing.

Tuesday: Day 10. Nothing.

Wednesday: The wait was over. I could now enter the property without an issue.

What I found inside illustrated that his definition of "clean" was faulty at best, as the following pictures show:

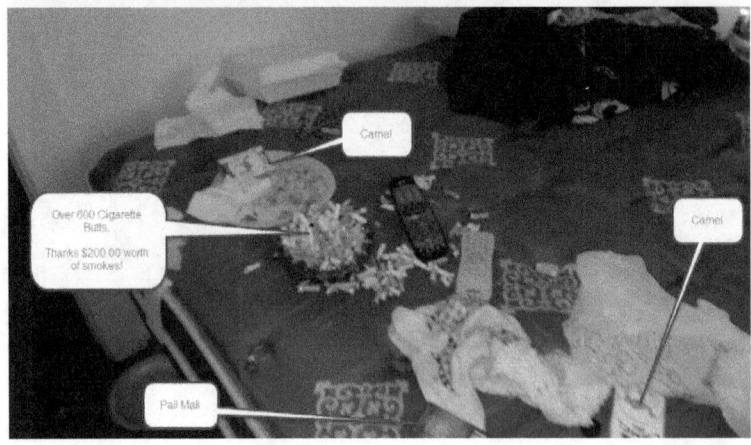

Cases of Empty Beer and multiple trash cans full of beer cans

"Clean," in this case, means he's taken what he wants and left the rest for me to clean up. There was no way he was getting his deposit back.

What he left also clearly showed what the tenant's priorities were. In three words: beer, cigarettes, and expediency.

While cleaning, I also found opened mail that showed he had signed up with the local cable provider. He had never paid a bill.

His electricity had not been paid in four months.

Apparently, the only bill he did pay was rent, until his cigarettes and beer took up too much of his money.

I ended up taking the tenant to small claims for unpaid rent and for cleaning. The case is still pending. The local sheriff has been unable to serve the tenant. As you can imagine, he did not leave a forwarding address.

I was glad I followed the letter of the law regarding the "10-Day Notice to Quit." If you need a set of rental forms, visit www.realtenanthistory.com and check out the forms packages.

8 – The Barter System

Some people will do anything to get out of paying rent. With our combined 40+ years of managing rental properties, we have been offered all kinds of "other" payments in place of actual money. Here are a few examples of what we've been offered:

1. Food Stamp Card
2. Sexual favors
3. Drugs
4. Stolen Property
5. Free labor

Food Stamp Card

Let's start with the food stamp incident.

About 10 years ago, I had a tenant who was usually a few days late with his rent. She always paid, just late.

One week when I stopped by to collect the rent, she told me, "It's been a bad week. I've had some unexpected bills. I don't have the rent yet." As usual, rent was at the bottom of her list of bills to pay.

"You've been consistently late for a long time. I can't help you this time." I wasn't trying to be mean, but I had bills I needed to pay as well.

"I have a food stamp card," she said, desperate. "It has $400 on it. I'll give it to you in exchange for the rent." She owed $200, so she was giving it to me for 50 cents on the dollar. "I have nowhere to go, and I don't know what'll happen to my kids if I get kicked out of here."

Normally, I would not agree to the exchange, but she was crying and going on in such a pitiful manner that I finally agreed.

"I'll take it this time. But if you're late again, I'll have to file for an immediate possession hearing."

I now had a $400 food stamp card in my pocket, so I headed to the local grocery store.

I wasn't quite sure what to do with the money. I didn't feel right spending it on myself. I decided to buy some items the tenant and her kids might need.

The total came to $417.83. I handed the cashier the card. After running it, the cashier leaned toward me and whispered, "I'm sorry, but the total is more than what's on the card."

"That's fine." I handed her a $20 bill. I then returned to the apartment to deliver the groceries to the tenant.

Now, was what I did legal? I don't think it was, but I didn't really want to evict the tenant, and I couldn't bear the family going without groceries for the rest of the month.

It's worth asking, did the grocery clerk check my ID? No, she did not. When was the last time you used a credit or debit card and had someone ID you?

Sexual Favors

Yes, this happened.

Again, I was collecting weekly rent from a tenant, and she did not have rent. "Maybe there's something I could do in exchange for the rent?" she suggested.

"You mean, like some work?"

"Not exactly. You see, my last landlord...sometimes instead of rent, he'd just ask for...."

Never mind how the conversation went. "No," I said firmly. To lighten the mood a bit, I added, "Maybe you can take that idea down to the electric company to pay your electric bill."

In this case, the tenant offered sexual favors, but in far more cases, landlords suggest it. At that point, the landlord has crossed a dangerous line.

A news story posted on Wavy.com, the news site for WAVY-TV News Channel 10 in Virginia, tells of how landlord Camilo B. Delfinado, 71, was arrested for at least two attempts to trade rent for sexual favors.

One tenant involved in the charges said she hadn't felt safe since she moved in. "I've basically been hiding from him since I moved here," she said. When she tried to talk to Delfinado about her eviction, he refused to talk about it.

The other tenant claimed Delfinado sexually harassed her in front of her three-year-old child.

Delfinado had been arrested six times previously on charges of sexual battery.

As this unfortunate event illustrates, a landlord's role is to provide a safe environment for his tenants. Any unwanted sexual advances will get him into deep trouble.

Drugs

I have a section in my lease that strictly prohibits illegal drugs on my properties. Still, occasionally, I'll have a tenant who's short on rent who offers me drugs in exchange.

The answer is no.

Then I typically go straight to the courthouse for an immediate possession hearing.

It's that simple.

Stolen Property

One time, I had a tenant who missed his monthly rent payment, so I went to his apartment and knocked on the door.

He opened the door a sliver. "What?"

"Your rent's late. I came to see if I could get it."

"I'll have it by the end of the week. I gotta sell some stuff first. Then you'll have it."

This intrigued me. "What are you selling?"

He opened the door to show me. There were stacks and stacks of electronic equipment.

I'd been keeping up with the local news, and I remembered a local electronics store had been burglarized earlier that week.

"That's a lot of stuff," I said. "Where'd you get it all?"

"A friend owed me some money. He gave me this stuff in exchange. You need anything? Maybe we can make a trade to lower the rent."

"No. I think I'm good."

I proceeded to the police station and let them handle it from there.

Working off Rent

This is the only item on the list that has actual merit. Depending on how a landlord's insurance is written and the skills a tenant might have, having a tenant do some work for you can be a benefit. Or it can be a huge mistake. Take such offers on a case-by-case basis, considering carefully if such an exchange is actually beneficial to both you and the tenant.

In the end, rent, on time, is best. But you already knew that.

9 – No Answer

What do you do when a tenant is avoiding you?

In my case, it was a tenant who was late paying his rent.

Every month I send out a late rent notice to all the tenants who missed their payment. This includes a statement that shows the rent plus the late fee. This month, I sent her a statement.

I waited a week. I checked the mail at the post office. No rent from this particular tenant.

I sent a second notice. It was now the 10th of the month. Rent was due on the 1st. After giving a couple days for the second notice to arrive, I followed up with a phone call. I got voice mail, so I left a message indicating I needed to hear from her in the next few days.

Nothing.

I decided to stop by the apartment. Typically, I try to stop by a tenant's apartment after dark so I can see if there are any lights on, or maybe a TV. Something to give an indication she was at home.

In this case, her car was in the parking area and the lights were on. I thought I'd catch her in the evening since she had an infant.

I knocked on the door, rang the doorbell, and waited almost 10 minutes for someone to answer the door.

No luck!

Even though I knew she was home, I had not given notice that I would be stopping by, so I did not enter the premises uninvited.

Over the next week, I noticed the dumpster quickly filling up. She seemed to be boxing up items and preparing to move.

I tried more phone calls, text messages, and even snail mail. No response.

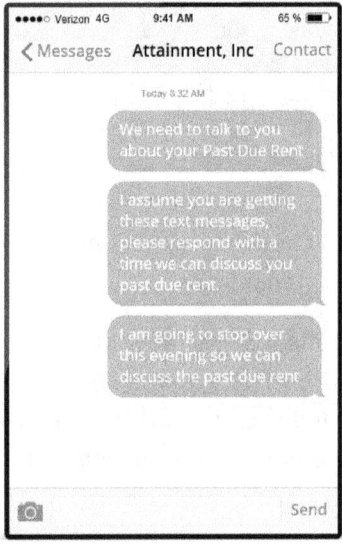

I asked the neighbor to keep an eye open for the tenant-in-question.

Rent was almost three weeks late now. The neighbor said the tenant was moving furniture. It was mid-week, so I decided to give the tenant until the weekend to get things moved.

On Saturday, I stopped by the apartment. It looked as if she had moved. She had left furniture, clothes, and kitchen items behind, but most of the belongings were gone.

Since the tenant had not responded to any of my communication over the last three weeks, I figured she had abandoned the rental unit. I decided to change the locks.

That's when my troubles began.

On Monday, I received a phone call from the tenant's mother. "Why have you changed the locks?" she asked angrily. "You locked my daughter and granddaughter out of their apartment!"

I tried to explain that I had been trying to contact the tenant for more than three weeks with no luck.

In return, she called me every name in the book.

"I'm sorry," I said. "You're not the tenant, so I can't discuss this issue with you." I hung up.

I found out later, though, that the *real* reason she had called was to find out if I was home. While I was on the phone, her husband and daughter broke into the apartment, grabbed the rest of the items they wanted, and proceeded to *trash* the rental unit.

I discovered this when I returned to the apartment Monday evening to get the unit ready for the next tenant.

I had pictures from when she moved in and pictures from when I changed the locks. Now I took a third set of pictures to show the damage done when they broke into the rental unit.

It took nearly a week to prepare the unit for rent and to determine the total cost that I would charge the tenant.

When someone moves suddenly like this, it can be hard to get a forwarding address. This tenant obviously didn't want me to know where she was moving to. However, I knew where she worked, so I used her work address as her forwarding address and sent the bill there.

Security Deposit Notice to Tenant - Termination of Tenancy

Forwarding Address:

Sent August 13, 2012

You must respond to this notice by mail within 7 days after receipt of same, otherwise you will forfeit the amount claimed for damages.

In _ July 21st, 2012_____, your occupancy of the premises commomly known as _____, Kendallville, IN 46755 terminated pursuant to statute, this notice is given to advise you of the items charged against your security deposit as follows:

(A)	Rent Deposit			$325.00
(B)	Pet Deposit	$_____ Less $_____ (Non Refundable)		
(C)	Key Deposit			$0
(D)	Net Deposit Refundable			($325.00)

Tenant Moved without notifying Landlord after 7 days

CHARGES AGAINST SECURITY DEPOSIT	Cost to Repair/Replace
1. General Cleaning (23 Hours @ $25) - Pictures Available	$ 575.00
2. Repair Broken Screens (1 Screens)	$ 90.00
3. Carpet Cleaning	$ 134.36
4. Replace blinds (4 Blinds @ $28 per)	$ 112.00
5. Repaint Apartment (Drawing on Walls and Screws) (4 Gal/7 Hours)	$ 275.00
6. Repair Holes in Walls	$ 487.00
7.	$ -
8.	$ -
9.	$ -

(E)	Total Damages		$1,673.36
(F)	Unpaid Rent	May-$225, June $325, July Thru 20th $216	$ 766.00
(G)	Other Charges	*Rent Through end of Lease	
		Court Charges $99.00	
		Late Fees $ 225.00	
		Late Fees $ -	
		Other $____ Explain _____	$324.00
(H)	Total Charges against security deposit	(E) plus (F) plus (G)	$2,763.36
(I)	Refund of Rent From ____ to ____ @ $____ per day		$0.00
	BALANCE	(D) minus (H) Plus (I)	($2,438.36)

If Positive Balance Due You *** Check Enclosed ***
If Negative-Amount Due us *** Please pay within 7 days *** If Payment not received within 7 days, this Matter will be turned over to our Attorney.

Ramit Payment to :

Date_____ Signed by:_____

In the county where this unit is, I could either have a small claims notice delivered via certified mail or have the local sheriff deliver it. Sheriff delivery is more expensive, but in this case it was well worth it.

At the small claim hearing, she did not show up. Summary judgment for the total amount claimed: $2,438.36 plus $975.34 in attorney fees. My attorney filed a wage garnishment hearing. She did not show up for that, either.

As of the writing of this chapter, I am receiving a little more than $50 a week.

10 – Reporting to the Credit Bureau

We all know tenants don't always make their rent payments on time. (Or at all.) Did you know these late payments don't necessarily affect a tenant's credit history? If you want to ensure that they do, you need to take the proper steps with the credit bureaus.

There are three major credit bureaus in the U.S., Experian, Equifax, and TransUnion. Each keeps its own consumer credit database and to report to these bureaus costs you time and money.

First, you have to become a customer of the credit bureau's reporting services. Only then can you report late rent payments.

The trick, however, is that each bureau operates independently. If you want to report late rental payments to each, you need to become a customer of all three bureaus.

According to Experian, a landlord has to pay subscriber fees and acquire the equipment necessary to report electronically to the bureau before he can use any of Experian's services. This software can cost as much as $600 per user (non-recurring), on top of a monthly service bureau fee.

As you can see, the cost of reporting to a credit bureau can be more hassle than it's worth. Federal law does not require you to report tenant credit information and similar types of "alternative credit" isn't widely reported.

If you do decide to report late rent payments to a credit bureau, though, you must also adhere to the Fair Credit Reporting Act, which basically requires that reporting be accurate, that you respond to consumer disputes about the information reported, and that certain fines apply for violating a consumer's rights. It also limits what information can be shared without a consumer's permission.

Despite all these requirements, in some cases it may be worth jumping through the hoops. By recording a tenant's late rent with the credit bureaus, you create a record of payments owed. You are holding the tenant responsible for his debt, and one day you may collect the debt owed you. If a past tenant wants to obtain a loan in his future, and you've reported his late rent, he will need to pay you to clean up his credit report.

If that happens, everyone wins.

Some information taken from
http://homeguides.sfgate.com/landlords-report-late-rent-credit-reports-61203.html

11 – Taken to Small Claims Court

Every once in a while when a tenant isn't happy with his landlord, he'll take him to small claims. This has happened to me only once.

In 2008, I had a single mother move into one of my apartments. Let's call her Becky. Becky lived there from June 2008 to January 2010. Her rent was late every month, but it *was* paid every month.

When she decided to move, she did not give any notice. I only found out because one of the other tenants called and asked about the apartment for a friend. Since Becky was on a month-to-month auto-renew lease, I didn't really care she hadn't given any notice.

The apartment was in decent shape, with only a few minor items to be charged against her deposit. On the next page is the "Termination of Tenancy Report" we sent her.

I owed Becky $278.55 from her deposit. I enclosed a check with the report. I figured everything was good.

A week later I received a letter from Becky indicating she was refusing the check. She believed I should have sent her the entire deposit. I responded to her letter by explaining that the damages were more than just wear and tear, and that was the reason for the deductions.

Security Deposit Notice to Tenant - Termination of Tenancy

Forwarding Address:

You must respond to this notice by mail within 7 days after receipt of same, otherwise you will forfeit the amount claimed for damages.

In __January 2010_____, your occupancy of the premises commomly known as _____ terminated pursuant to statute, this notice is given to advise you of the items charged against your security deposit as follows:

(A) Rent Deposit — $525.00
(B) Pet Deposit $_____ Less $_____ (Non Refundable)
(C) Key Deposit — $0
(D) Net Deposit Refundable — ($525.00)

Tenant Moved without notifying Landlord after 7 days

CHARGES AGAINST SECURITY DEPOSIT — Cost to Repair/Replace
1. Carpet Cleaning 3 Rooms — $ 96.45
2. General Cleaning (4 Hours @ 25.00) — $ 100.00
3. Painting (2 Hours @ 25.00) — $ 50.00
4. — $ -
5. — $ -
6. — $ -
7. — $ -
8. — $ -
9. — $ -

(E) Total Damages — $246.45
(F) Unpaid Rent — $ -
(G) Other Charges
    Court Charges $0.00
    Late Fees $ -
    Other $_____ Explain _____ $0.00
(H) Total Charges against security deposit — (E) plus (F) plus (G) $246.45
(I) Refund of Rent From _____ to _____ @ $____ per day — $0.00

BALANCE — (D) minus (H) Plus (I) **$278.55**

If Positive Balance Due You *** Check Enclosed ***
If Negative-Amount Due us *** **Please pay within 7 days** *** **If Payment not received within 7 days, this Matter will be turned over to our Attorney.**

Remit Payment to:

Date _____ Signed by: _____

I heard nothing from her until the county sheriff delivered a court document saying that Becky had filed a claim against both me and my wife.

A month later I appeared in court. My wife was unable to attend. When the case was called, I sat in the defendant's seat. Becky and her father were in the plaintiffs' seats.

I listened as Becky told her side of the story, which took about 10 minutes. Then the judge turned to me. "Do you have anything to say?"

"I'd just like to say that neither I nor my wife ever rented to the plaintiff."

You can imagine the look on Becky's face when I said this. "You're lying!" she said. Her father chimed in as well. "He's the one who rented to her!"

"Please be quiet. It's the defendant's turn to speak," the judge explained. "You will have another chance to speak later." He addressed me again. "What do you mean that you never rented to the plaintiff?"

"I own a company, Attainment, Inc., that rented the apartment to Becky, but neither my wife nor I personally rented her the apartment. I'm being charged as an individual, not as a corporation, so I do not think this case has any merit."

The judge turned to Becky. "Is this true?"

"It is."

"Case dismissed with prejudice."

As I walked out of the courtroom, I asked Becky if she'd like me to resend the check for $278.55. Her father interrupted. "If she isn't getting the entire deposit back, she doesn't want any of it."

I felt bad that she was taking advice from someone who knew nothing about the law, but there wasn't anything I could do about it.

Now, it's vital that a landlord understand that if he gets taken to small claims by a tenant while the tenant is still occupying the rental unit, the landlord should not retaliate in any way toward the tenant.

I didn't have to worry, since Becky had already moved out, but it's a good thing to keep in mind.

Different states have different statues dealing with landlord retaliation. Here are a few examples.

Indiana

No statute.

Ohio

A landlord may not retaliate against a tenant by increasing rent, decreasing services, or bringing or threatening eviction because the tenant has:

- complained to an appropriate governmental agency of a building, housing, health, or safety code violation;
- complained to the landlord of conditions that violate Landlord Obligations as defined in §§ 5321.05;
- or joined with other tenants to negotiate or deal collectively with the landlord on any terms or conditions of a rental agreement.
- Tenant may use any retaliatory action by the landlord as a defense to an eviction, to recover possession of the premises or to terminate the rental agreement. (§§ 5321.02)

Illinois

The Retaliatory Eviction Act reads:

Sec. 1. It is declared to be against the public policy of the State for a landlord to terminate or refuse to renew a lease or tenancy of property used as a residence on the ground that the tenant has complained to any governmental authority of a bona fide violation of any applicable building code, health ordinance, or similar regulation. Any provision in any lease, or any agreement or understanding, purporting to permit the landlord to terminate or refuse to renew a lease or tenancy for such reason is void.

Kentucky

A landlord must not terminate, refuse to renew a lease, or fine a tenant for complaining to the landlord for a violation listed under KRS § 383.595 for complaining to a government agency, or being involved in a tenant's organization, otherwise retaliation will be assumed. (KRS§ 383.705).

~~~

As you can see, it is always best to act aboveboard whenever a tenant takes a complaint to a higher authority.

The exact regulations in each state are different, however, so if you need specifics for a state in which you own rental units, contact Real Tenant History for additional information.

12 – Smoke 'Em If You Got 'Em

Newsflash! Tenants that smoke will eventually have cigarette burns in their carpet. Hopefully, it's just the carpet that gets burnt....

In early 1996, I purchased two side-by-side duplexes. The properties were in bad condition, so I chose the best two tenants and put them in one duplex while I renovated the other.

The renovation took about four months. I replaced the siding and the roof. I installed a new porch. I redid everything inside, taking it down to studs and wood floors. I put in new kitchens, new bathrooms, new drywall, new everything.

By late summer, I had moved the two tenants into the newly renovated apartments so I could work on the other duplex.

When the tenant I'll call Veronica moved into the lower unit, she was ecstatic. She had never rented such a nice apartment. It was far nicer than she was used to. She rented from me until Summer 2001.

When she moved out, I inspected the apartment. What I found terrified me. Next to her bed were more than 200 cigarette burns, some three inches long.

Oh, what could have happened when she had dropped one of those cigarettes when she fell asleep!

Visions of the duplex on fire went through my mind for weeks. I was glad nothing had happened, but I wanted to be sure to prevent anything happening in the future as well.

I decided we were going to do things different from now on.

First, a few facts about the temperature of a lit cigarette. When not drawing, the lit portion is between 752-1112 degrees

Fahrenheit (400-580 degrees Celsius). When one draws, the temperature rises to 1292 degrees Fahrenheit (700 degrees Celsius).

These numbers are average readings from a standard FE-CuNi digital thermocouple thermometer.

This tells me one thing I already knew: cigarettes are fire hazards.

To lessen that risk, the first thing I did was supply a letter to all new tenants. It reads like this:

~~~

Sensible Approach

As a tenant, you need to be aware that no matter what steps you take, there is always a chance of fire. You need to keep exits accessible and operational and make sure evacuation procedures are in place.

You can also reduce the risk of fire in the following ways:

- *Smoke Detectors* – Smoke detectors may not prevent fire, but early detection may reduce the damage and save lives.
- *Smoking* – <u>Never</u> smoke in bed or while dozing on the couch. Empty ashtrays regularly and keep paper and other flammable materials away from them.
- *Dryer* – Clear the lint filter every time you use the dryer.
- *Power Outlets* – Don't overload your power outlets or power strips.
- *Heaters* – Use safe heating methods and don't dry clothes on your heater in the winter.
- *Matches* – Keep matches and lighters away from children.
- *Stove tops* – Keep kitchen towels away from stove tops. Never leave a boiling saucepan unattended.

- *Grills* – Grills are a common source of house fires even though they are outside. Keep your grill safe and maintain your propane tank.
- *Wiring* – Domestic wiring needs to be checked and replaced if faulty.
- *Bushfires* – If you live in a bushfire prone area, make sure you follow proper guidelines and maintenance.
- *Fire extinguishers* – We have provided a fire extinguisher at this rental unit. Use it if necessary, and inform us if it has been used.

~~~

In addition to providing the above information, I also perform an inspection at least twice a year. During these inspections, I make an effort to enforce the checklist above.

Hazards and Statistics

What are the chances of having a fire in a rental unit?

According to a 2006 report from the U.S. Fire Administration, 3,245 civilians were killed in fires that year, 81% of which occurred in residences. There were 16,400 civilians injured in fires, and 106 firefighters lost their lives while on duty. Fire killed more Americans than all natural disasters combined. People reported 1.6 million fires that caused more than $11 billion in direct property damage.

The majority of fire-related deaths are due to smoke inhalation. Even if someone escapes the flames, he may still die from carbon monoxide poisoning.

Fire risks increase during the holiday season due to dried-out Christmas trees, increased use of candles, electrical decorations, and frequent cooking and baking.

Fire extinguishers should be easily accessible throughout the rental unit, particularly in areas most prone to fires. Everyone in the unit should be able to use it. The National Fire Protection Association uses the acronym PASS to teach people how to use a fire extinguisher:

- **P**ull the pin. Release the lock with the nozzle pointing away from you.
- **A**im low. Point the extinguisher at the base of the fire.
- **S**queeze the lever slowly and evenly.
- **S**weep the nozzle from side to side."

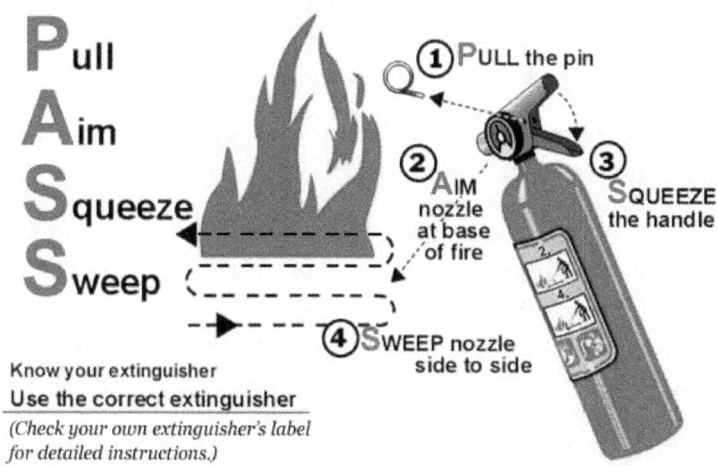

Reducing the Risk

Knowing these statistics, it's worth spending time reducing the risk of fire in a rental unit.

A typical fire hazard is when drapery or other furnishing comes in contact or close proximity with electrical appliances such as lights and heaters. The continuous radiation of heat from these sources can cause the furnishing to burst into flames. By moving flammable objects away from these heat sources and by turning off or unplugging the heat sources when not in use, you can easily reduce your risk of fire.

If a rental unit depends on a wood stove for heat, a screen, preferably without perforations, should enclose the area so sparks or embers cannot exit the fireplace.

You can also use a fire-retardant spray on curtains, carpets, bedding, paper and wood products, decorations, and other in-unit objects.

Fire gels can also be applied to the property. Areas surrounded by brush have a greater risk of fire damage, so gels can help protect these areas from spreading fire.

While these products do not perfectly prevent fires, they greatly reduce the ability of a fire to start.

After a fire, it can be an ordeal to remove the charred remains from the unit. Often, a police marshal must be consulted before you can fully rid the unit of the fire's remains. It is much better to channel efforts into fire prevention so that this is never an issue.

While it is wise to equip rental units with fire alarms, fire extinguishers, and sprinkler systems, preventing a fire before it happens should be your primary concern. A little effort now to inspect the unit for fire risk can greatly reduce the chance of the tragedy and loss caused by a fire.

Do it now!

13 – Meth Labs: A Rental Owner's Nightmare

If there's one kind of notice you don't want to see posted on one of your properties, it's this:

This Property Is CONDEMNED!

But if the property housed a meth lab, that's exactly what you *will* see.

Laws, of course, vary from state to state and often from county to county. Some counties will condemn a property outright. Others will declare an abatement. Such matters are generally turned over to the local health department.

In Noble County, Indiana, where I have properties, law requires any residence in which methamphetamine was produced must be declared unfit for human occupancy until it's been tested and found free of hazardous chemicals.*

And the cleanup? It often winds up as your responsibility. It's no picnic and it's not cheap.

It can cost up to $20,000 to clean up a rental unit after it's been contaminated with meth residue. It's no surprise, then, that so many of these structures are simply torn down. Here are the relevant statistics for Noble County, Indiana, and its surrounding counties:

Meth Condemnations in 2013 by County

County	Total Condemned	Total Torn Down	% Torn Down
Noble County	40	16	40.00%
Dekalb County	17	5	29.41%

Lagrange County	13	5	38.46%
Steuben County	7	3	42.86%

During the process of condemnation and cleanup (or teardown), state police make periodic checks to ensure all signage is properly posted. The signs cannot be removed until the local health department has tested, inspected, and passed the property.

Clearly, having a meth lab on your rental property is a nightmare! But are meth labs so common that you should be worried?

Unfortunately, the answer is yes. Take a look at these latest available DEA statistics from the U.S. Department of Justice:

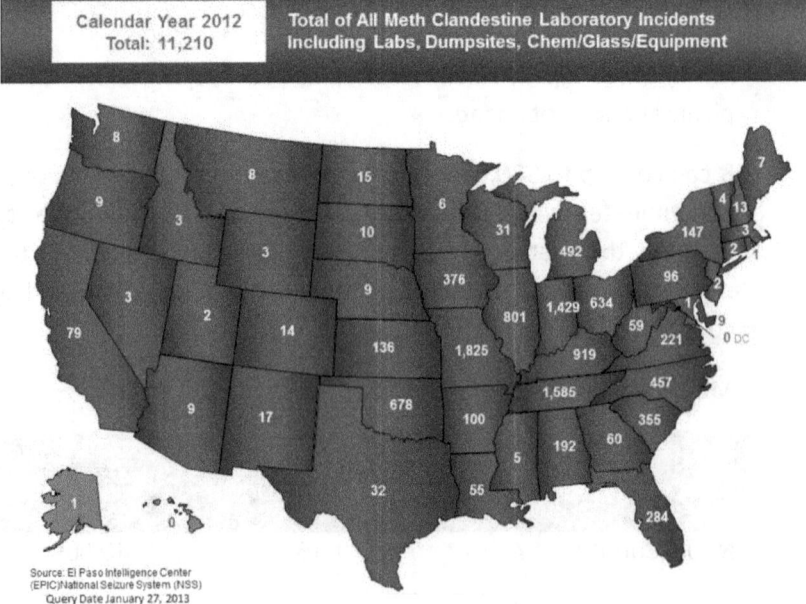

Source: http://www.justice.gov/dea/resource-center/meth-lab-maps.shtml

As the map shows, lots of people are cooking up meth on the sly—often in states you might not expect! And these are just the incidents we know about.

Maybe your state's number is low enough that you don't feel it necessary to take precautions. But do you really want to chance it?

Meth labs have been discovered in hotel and motel rooms, restaurants, barns, private homes and apartments, storage facilities, fields, vacant buildings, and vehicles. People intent on producing meth are cagey, secretive, and determined. No type of property is immune.

Effects of Meth Chemicals

Then there are these facts to consider, most of which we've garnered from www.meth-kills.org/meth-lab.html.

A minimum of five to seven pounds of chemical waste is produced for each pound of meth manufactured. Many of the chemicals involved in meth production are highly toxic.

The health effects of exposure to meth lab chemicals depend on the lab process, the type and amount of chemicals used, the length of exposure, and the age and health of those exposed.

Meth chemicals can enter the body by being breathed in, ingested, or absorbed through the skin. It doesn't take long for damage to occur. Even short exposure to the chemicals can cause shortness of breath, coughing, chest pain, lack of coordination, chemical irritation, and burns to the skin, eyes, nose, and mouth.

Less severe symptoms include headaches, nausea, dizziness, and fatigue.

Even those who aren't drug users can suffer the consequences of acute exposure while or immediately after making methamphetamine.

In some cases, exposure to these chemicals can lead to death.

Do you really want to clean up after a meth producer?

Insidious Side Effects of Meth Labs

The sad truth is that children are frequently victims of meth labs, and they can suffer from more than the symptoms listed above, as stories from the Meth-Kills website show.

Improperly mixed meth chemicals can explode. When authorities responded to one such explosion, they found an 11-month-old baby still clinging to life in the home lab's burning wreckage. The parents had fled, leaving the child behind.

The authorities rushed the infant to the hospital, but it had already suffered serious harm. The infant died a few months later.

The fugitive parents were eventually captured while attempting to purchase chemicals to make more meth.

In another instance, officers found a meth lab in the bedroom of a one-year-old child. The child was in the room, in his walker, at the time of the raid.

The officers took the child into custody. Multiple charges were filed against the parents, including child desertion.

In a third case, narcotics officers conducting a probation search of a residence discovered that the woman living there had been making meth in a travel trailer parked on the property. The officers found her four-year-old daughter playing outside by some meth waste.

During an interrogation, the girl described and drew pictures of a smoking pipe made of glass. She also talked about domestic violence she had witnessed in the home.

Not only was her mother charged with meth manufacture, but also child endangerment, as well as other charges. The daughter, after being taken to the hospital and testing positive for meth and other drugs, was placed in a foster home.

These are sad stories. You can avoid having such tragedies play out on your rental properties by knowing what to look for.

How to Recognize the Signs of a Meth Lab

Unless you stumble on a meth lab while it's cooking, the signs of its existence aren't likely to jump out at you. Meth producers are nothing if not secretive.

Besides that, the ingredients to make meth, which is a white, crystalline powder, or crystal meth, which consists of clear chunks resembling ice, are mostly household ingredients. When they're mixed together and cooked, however, the resultant toxic chemical residue can remain on room surfaces for months or years afterward.

Meth labs can quickly become hazardous chemical waste sites, exposing anyone who comes in contact with them to harmful health effects as well as creating the potential for fires and explosions.

Many meth labs must be evacuated and cleaned by hazardous waste professionals.

Here is a list of the most common signs of a rental property meth lab, followed by the most common supplies needed for a meth lab:

- The windows are blacked out.
- You smell a strong odor of solvents.
- There are iodine- or chemical-stained fixtures in bathrooms or kitchens.
- A travel trailer or RV is parked on the property.
- The tenants show increased activity, especially at night.
- The accumulation of excessive trash.

The Most Common Meth Lab Supplies

- Over-the-counter cold and asthma medications. Typical brands including Sudafed® and old-formula Mini Thin®

Energy Boosters, which contain ephedrine or pseudoephedrine as decongestants or stimulants.

- Ephedrine or pseudoephedrine tablets
- Mason jars
- Propane tanks
- Lithium batteries
- Plastic tubing
- Funnels
- Glass containers
- Red-stained coffee filters
- Empty pill bottles
- Empty cans of toluene, alcohol, or paint thinner
- Ammonia
- Camp stove fuel

- Starter fluid
- Rock Salt with iodine
- Hydrogen peroxide

Diligence: the Necessary Requirement for Keeping Properties Meth Lab Free

By staying alert for these signs and supplies, you can recognize a potential meth lab before it's too late. Being aware can go a long way toward helping you keep your properties clean and constantly producing revenue.

Another step you can take is to visit RealTenantHistory.com. Its T.I.L.E. (Tenant Information Landlord Evaluation) reviews will show you whether tenant prospects have had previous issues with meth so you can avoid renting to them in the first place.

~~~

*Check your own state laws for what constitutes a meth-contaminated property. Indiana's definition may be found at www.in.gov/legislative/iac/T03180/A00010.PDF. A few highlights of this document include:

> "(b) For an apartment building, multifamily dwelling, condominium, hotel, or motel, the term ['contaminated property'] is limited to the unit that was identified by the law enforcement agency as having been used for the illegal manufacture of a controlled substance if all of the following are true:
>
> - The entry to the unit is located on the:
>   - outside of the structure; or
>   - interior of the structure and is closed by a fire door assembly.
> - The unit has no other opening to another unit or space.
> - The heating, ventilating, and air conditioning system for that unit is enclosed within that unit and is separate from the heating, ventilating, and air conditioning system of any other unit, except for:

- a hot water boiler that serves more than one (1) unit in the structure; or

- an air conditioning condenser located outside the structure.

(c) The property is not a contaminated property if the law enforcement agency that identifies the property as having been used for the illegal manufacture of a controlled substance determines that:

- The process used to manufacture the controlled substance has not been started;

- All chemicals to be used in the illegal manufacture of the controlled substance have been removed; and

- No contamination related to the illegal manufacture of a controlled substance is present.

(d) The term includes any areas outside a structure that were used for the disposal of chemicals used in the illegal manufacture of a controlled substance.

(e) A property is no longer a contaminated property when the certificate of decontamination prepared under 318 IAC 1-5-9 for that property has been issued or the activities required by 318 IAC 1-6-2 have been completed. (Department of Environmental Management; 318 IAC 1-2-8; filed Feb 21, 2007, 1:56 p.m.: 20070321-IR-318060125FRA; readopted filed Aug 5, 2013, 2:08 p.m.: 20130904-IR-318130240RFA)

14 – Contractor Speak

If you ever work with a contractor, you'll learn that—in most cases—a contractor speaks a foreign language. This "contractor speak" is important for property owners and landlords to understand. With a bit of practice, and the memorization of a few key phrases, all of us can begin to understand this strange tongue. In the long run, it will clear up confusion, misunderstandings, and embarrassing looks of utter bewilderment.

Lesson 1 – Cubic Yards

This is landscaper jargon. Whether they are dealing with top soil, landscaping mulch, decorative stone, or any other material, a landscaper will inescapably utter the words, "We'll need such-and-such cubic yards of peat moss," or something similar.

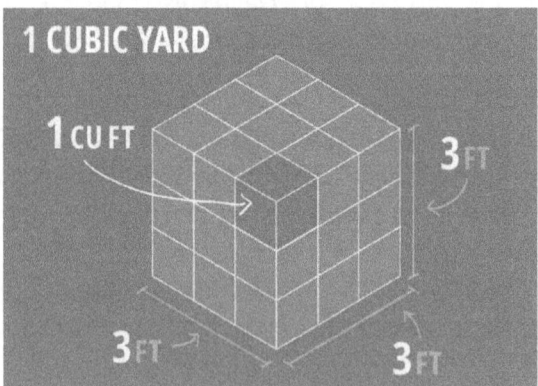

When you visualize a cubic yard, think of three to four full wheelbarrows. That will alleviate your confusion. Now when you hear, "We'll need four cubic yards of top soil," you know the landscaper means you'll need about 12-16 wheelbarrows of dirt.

Lesson 2 – Square Yard vs. Square Feet

Not so long ago, I could buy carpet and padding, and even hardwood flooring, by the square yard. However, as prices rose, the industry changed the measurement to square feet to "lower" the price.

While there are some flooring stores that still know what you mean when you utter the antiquated words, "square yards," just as some people still know what you mean when you say "rotary phone," most prefer to deal in square feet now.

The times, they are a-changin'.

If you need to convert from square yards to square feet, just multiply by nine.

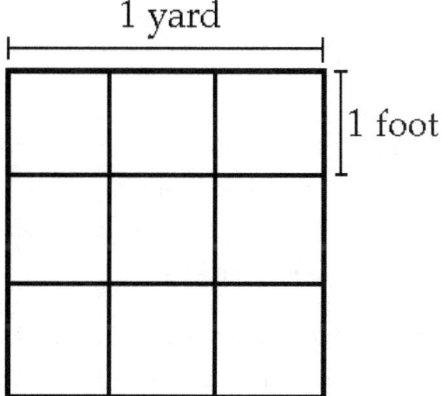

Lesson 3 – Squares

Everything a roofing contractor says seems to include the word "squares." Whether they are discussing rolled roofing, shingles, or felt papers, it's always "squares."

Translation—a square is 100 square feet. Simple enough.

Lesson 4 – Change Order

When getting a quote from a contractor, be sure to clearly explain what you want done, and make sure the quote provided is detailed enough that you know exactly what the contractor is providing in both labor estimates and material estimates.

If communication is unclear at this point and the contractor later finds the work is taking either more labor or more materials than expected, you will receive a "change order."

This change order is a bill that helps the contractor recoup the costs incurred by the unforeseen extra materials or labor. If you think the change order is unfair, don't sign it. You can still negotiate with the contractor for a better price.

Lesson 5 – Electrical Service

When an electrician brings up your "electrical service," he is referring to everything that has electricity running through it, from the power lines attached to your property to the electrical meter to the circuit breaker panel or fuse box.

Once he reaches the circuit panel, or fuse box in older residences, he might start throwing around the term AMP. Most fuse boxes in older properties only support 60 AMP service. Newer constructions with circuit panels support somewhere between 100 and 200 AMPs of service.

Lesson 6 – Clean Out

This is plumber lingo. Basically, a clean out is access to a

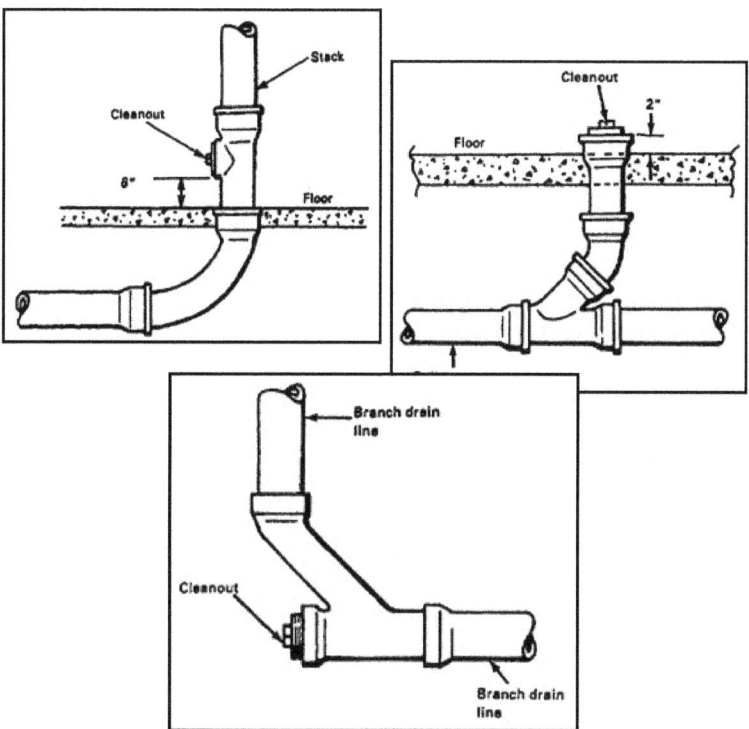

plumbing drain pipe.

Almost all properties have at least one clean out for clearing out debris in the waste water lines. It can be inside or outside. Most commonly, a property has one main clean out four to six inches in diameter, along with smaller clean outs under sinks, tubs, and showers.

When having a sewer line worked on outside a property with no outdoor clean out, I highly recommend spending a little extra to have an outdoor clean out installed.

Conclusion

Once you've mastered these few simple phrases, you will be well on your way to truly speaking like a contractor! Congratulations!

15 – Making Carpet Last

When I purchased my first rental property more than 20 years ago, I decided to start a strategic relationship with a local carpet and upholstery cleaner. I knew I didn't have the tools, time, or expertise to clean carpets when tenants moved out.

Back in those Pre-Internet days, I pulled out the yellow pages and called all the carpet cleaning companies in the area. After talking with a half dozen companies, I found two I liked. I gave them each a test job. I had each one clean a different apartment, then checked the carpets at four and eight weeks after to see how the cleaning had held up.

From this test, I decided to go with Phend's Carpet and Upholstery.

Since I've had a great relationship with the company for the past 20 years, I asked Lynn Phen if he would put together some tips for property managers and landlords. What follows is from what he provided me.

Carpet is an expensive investment, and there are ways to reduce carpet replacement costs.

Before you purchase carpet, though, you need to purchase carpet padding. Do not overlook this. Carpet padding is the foundation of your carpet and is necessary to support and cushion the carpet. The protection it provides is worth the expense.

Good carpet padding will outlast the carpet, so it can be reused when the carpet is replaced. Some padding is made specifically for stain resistance, while others focus on comfort and softness. Some padding works to prevent molds and can be good for areas with high moisture.

After the padding, comes the carpet. Keep in mind that neutral colors like tans and light browns are good choices. They blend with most colors and décor. Also, if you allow pets, choosing a carpet with a spotty texture or design is a good idea. Visit a local carpet retailer for samples and ideas.

When purchasing carpet for a rental unit, choose one that can endure normal wear and tear well. Then consider how frequently you plan to replace the carpet.

Lower-grade carpets are a good option if you plan to replace the carpets often due to heavy wear and tear or if you allow pets. A middle- or high-grade carpet is a better choice if you do not allow pets and expect tenants not to be rough on the carpet. It'll cost more upfront because it should last longer.

Remember, purchasing high-end carpet is not necessarily a good idea. Every tenant has his own idea of carpet cleanliness and heavy foot traffic is possible. You need to balance quality with the reality of potential wear and tear.

Reducing soil accumulation will keep carpets clean longer. Encourage your tenants to use mats or runners. Regular vacuuming keeps dirt from settling into the carpet. When a tenant moves, immediately work to remove spots to keep them from becoming permanent stains.

The information below is from a brochure that Phend's Carpet Cleaning and Upholstery put together for their customers.

1. **Reduce soil accumulation.** Use wipe-off mats at all entrances to keep outside soil from being tracked onto the carpet. You may want to relocate furniture periodically to allow for an even distribution of traffic and wear on the carpet. Mats and runners will reduce wear in heavy traffic areas. If your carpet is not wall to wall, rotate it occasionally to reduce wear.
2. **Vacuum regularly.** Whoever said "The three best ways to clean carpet are vacuum, vacuum, vacuum" was a carpet expert. Most soil, even dust, is in the form of hard particles. When left in the carpet, these gritty, sharp-edged particles abrade the pile as effectively as sandpaper. Regular and thorough vacuuming will remove them. How frequently should you vacuum? That depends on the amount of traffic and soiling to which your carpet is exposed. If you have "average" conditions, use Guide B...and make adjustments to meet your own needs.
    i. **Guide A (Light traffic areas)** Vacuum twice weekly in traffic lanes. Vacuum the entire area once each week.
    ii. **Guide B (Medium to heavy traffic lanes)** Vacuum traffic lanes at least once daily. Vacuum the entire area twice weekly.

Up to three passes of the machine is considered light cleaning; five to seven may be necessary for heavy cleaning. A vacuum cleaner or attachment with a rotating brush or "beater bar" to agitate the pile is more effective than one that relies on suction only. Be sure to pay attention to the correct pile-height adjustment for carpet.

3. **Remove spills immediately.** Anything spilled on carpet should be cleaned up promptly. Almost all spilled materials

will stain or discolor the carpet or increase soiling if left unattended.

Steps to remove spills

- Blot with a clean white cloth or clean white paper towel or scoop up as much of the spill as possible. Don't scrub.
- Find spill in Stain Removal Chart 1 (below) and follow the procedure.
- Apply all cleaning solutions sparingly. Do not get the carpet backing wet. Use a clean white cloth or apply directly to spot as directed in the Removal Procedure.
- Blot from outer edge of spill inward, toward center, to keep the spill from spreading.
- Blot up cleaning solution.
- Rinse sparingly with clear water on damp sponge.
- Blot thoroughly to remove cleaning solution. Rinse with water again if carpet feels sticky or soapy.
- Finish blotting by placing a ½" thick pad of clean white towel or white cloth over the spot. Press with a heavy weight for two hours or overnight. Get up all the moisture to prevent resoiling and bacteria growth.

Stain Removal Equipment

- Detergent – Diluted solution of mild hand-dishwashing detergent without oily skin conditioners.
- Ammonia – Undiluted household ammonia (containing detergent).
- Vinegar – Undiluted white vinegar.
- Solvent – Dry-cleaning solvent (spot remover).
- Dry Powder – i.e. Capture, Blue Luster, or Host.
- Blotting Material – White cloth, paper towels.

Keep these materials readily available as your carpet "First-Aid Kit." A medicine dropper or a plastic squeeze bottle of the type used for dispensing mustard, ketchup or some brands of hair coloring are convenient means of application. If you store your solutions in these bottles, be sure to label them. Keep them out of the reach of children.

WARNING: HOUSEHOLD CHEMICALS MAY "SPOT" YOUR CARPET

Many modern-day household chemicals serve to improve our lives; however, they may cause mysterious spots when they come in contact with carpet or other dyed fabrics. Depending on humidity and temperature, discolorations may not appear until several days after the carpet was exposed to the chemical. The stain-resistant properties of ANSO IV nylon cannot control such chemical reactions; therefore, the consumer must take precautions to prevent them. Here are some of the common culprits:

- Acne Medicines – Most skin care products contain benzoyl peroxide, which is a powerful oxidizing agent in the presence of humidity. Hand or facial residue can be unknowingly brushed onto carpet. It is recommended that a strong soap be used by the acne medicine user to make certain that the residue is not left on the face and hands.

- Household Cleaners – Tile, toilet bowl, drain, and oven cleaners contain strong acids or alkalis which can weaken the carpet fiber and cause "bleeding." Exercise caution when using these cleaners around carpeted areas.

- Bleaches – Chlorine and oxygen bleaches, mildew killers, and swimming pool chemicals, which can be tracked into the home by unknowing swimmers, will cause yellow spots.

- DMSO – Dimethysulfoxide, which is commonly used for pain relief medicines for arthritis, back problems, athletic injuries and muscular aches can cause rapid loss of color on carpet due to its solvent action.

- Insecticides and Pesticides – Products most often involved are Malathion, Diazinon, Vapona, and many others. When using indoors, apply insecticide in a fan-shaped mist and only to baseboards—never directly onto carpet.

- Plant Foods – Liquid plant food spills or leakage from flower pots can cause oxidation spots. These typically start near the carpet backing and progress to the carpet surface and is sometimes not apparent for months.

Prevention is the Key

Once a spot of discoloration on the carpet occurs, the damage is done, and carpet restoration or replacement may be necessary. If you know that one of these chemicals has been in contact with your carpet, consult a professional carpet cleaner to have the chemical extracted as soon as possible. Do not attempt to remove the chemical yourself. Your carpet is an expensive investment. Take the necessary precautions to ensure that it stays beautiful for a long time.

Stain Removal Chart 1

Stain	Procedure	Stain	Procedure
Asphalt	A	Lacquer	A
Beer	E	Lard	A
Berries	E	Linseed Oil	A
Blood	B	Machine Oil	A
Butter	A	Mascara	A
Candle Wax	G	Mayonnaise	B
Candy (Sugar)	D	Mercurochrome	E
Carbon Black	A	Menthloate	E
Charcoal	A	Milk	B
Cheese	B	Mimeo Correction Fluid	A
Chewing Gum	G	Mixed Drinks	E
Chocolate	B	Model Cement	L
Coffee	E	Mustard	E
Cooking Oil	A	Nail Polish	L
Crayon	A	Paint- Latex	A
Crème de Menthe	F	Paint- Oil	A
Dye- Blue, Black, Green	F	Rubber Cement	A
Dye- Red	E	Shellac	I
Earth	B	Shoe Polish	A
Egg	B	Shortening	A
Excrement	B	Soft Drinks	E
Fish Slime	B	Soy Sauce	B
Foundation Make-up	A	Starch	B
Fruit Juice	E	Tar	A
Furniture Polish	A	Tea	E
Furniture Polish with Stain	H	Tooth Paste	B
Gravy	A	Typewriter Ribbon	A
Hair Oil	A	Urine- Dry	J
Hand Lotion	A	Urine- Fresh	K
Ice Cream	B	Varnish	A
Ink- Ball Point	A	Vaseline	A
Ink- Fountain Pen	F	Vomit	C
Ink- India, Marking Pen	A	Wax- Paste	A
Ink- Mimeo	A	White Glue	B
Ketchup	B	Wine	E

	Removal Procedures	
Procedure A	**Procedure B**	**Procedure C**
Apply Solvent, Blot, Detergent, Blot, Water, Blot	Detergent, Blot, Ammonia, Blot, Detergent, Blot, White Vinegar, Blot, Water, Blot	Mix Baking Soda & Water, Apply, Scrape & Vacuum, Water, Blot, Enzyme Presoak, Cover with Aluminum Foil, Wait 30 Minutes and Blot, Water, Blot, Dry Powder Cleaning
Procedure D	**Procedure E**	**Procedure F**
Detergent, Blot, White Vinegar, Detergent, Blot, Water, Blot	Detergent, Blot, Ammonia, Blot, White Vinegar, Blot, Water, Blot, Dry Powder Cleaning	Detergent, Blot, White Vinegar, Blot, Ammonia, Blot, White Vinegar, Blot, Water, Blot
Procedure G	**Procedure H**	**Procedure I**
Freeze with Ice cube or Freon, Shatter with Blunt Object, Vacuum out Chips, Apply Solvent, Soak, Blot, Repeat, if necessary	Apply Solvent, Soak Several Minutes, Blot, Detergent, Blot, Water, Blot	Denatured Alcohol, Blot, Repeat, if necessary. Note: Pretest for dye bleeding.
Procedure J	**Procedure K**	**Procedure L**
Detergent, Blot, White Vinegar, Blot, Ammonia, Blot, Detergent, Blot, White Vinegar, Blot, Water, Blot	Blot, Water, Blot, Ammonia, Blot, Detergent, Blot, White Vinegar, Blot, Water, Blot	Polish Remover (Non-Oily if Possible), Blot, Repeat

16 – The Utility Trap

Most of my rental properties require the tenant to pay for utilities. These include water/sewer, electricity, and gas. I pay for the trash. There's a good reason for this.

I have a friend with some rental properties who used to make the tenants pay for trash disposal, until a certain tenant moved out.

This tenant was renting a two-bedroom apartment just for himself. Upon the termination of this tenant's lease at the end of the year, the tenant wanted to look for a bigger place so he and his girlfriend could move in together. When the tenant moved, my friend did not have time for a walkthrough, so the tenant just left the keys on the counter of the unit.

Well, my friend entered the property. He found it to be surprisingly clean. The kitchen was clean, the living room was spotless, the bathroom immaculate. But there was an odor. He kept looking through the house. He checked the first bedroom. Looking good.

He opened the door to the second bedroom—180 bags of trash. Odor found.

Apparently, it was easier to bag and store the trash in the spare bedroom than to pay for its disposal.

It took six trips to the dump to remove all the bags of trash. Needless to say, the spare bedroom's carpet was ruined.

Once the trash was removed, the carpet replaced, and the room cleaned, the apartment no longer smelled. After a coat of paint and a bit of general cleaning, it was ready to re-rent.

After this incident, my friend decided he would increase the rent a small amount to cover trash removal. Now he has a dumpster at each of his rental properties. The only thing a tenant needs to do is get the trash to the dumpster.

Dealing with utilities on a rental property can be confusing. Here are some typical questions I receive from other Independent Rental Owners (IROs):

1. Will a landlord be responsible for utilities if a tenant moves out?

2. Can a landlord disconnect the utilities of the property if the tenant is behind on his bills?

3. Can a landlord take the utilities out of a tenant's name?

4. Can a landlord call the utility companies and have them put into the new tenant's name?

The answers to these questions become clear once you understand the relationship between a landlord and the utility companies.

The first thing any IRO should do after purchasing a rental property is contact all utility service providers and let them know he is the owner of the property and that it will be used as a rental property.

After this is done, remember: Any utilities which are the tenant's responsibility *are the tenant's responsibility*.

If the tenant moves out, they must contact the utility company. The landlord cannot turn off the service.

If the tenant skips on the bill, it is still the tenant's responsibility. The landlord should inform the utility company that the tenant has moved. It is the utility company's responsibility to pursue the charges. The company will turn on the utility in the new tenant's name on request from the new tenant.

The only time a landlord would put a utility a tenant is responsible for in his name is when the unit is vacant. When the unit is rented again, the landlord can call the company, have the utility ended in his name, and have a final reading done.

Typically, utility companies give new tenants 8-10 days to get service into their name before cutting off service. I give the tenants three days to put utilities in their names. Otherwise, they are in violation of the lease and will receive a letter indicating this.

Finally, as a landlord, you cannot disconnect a utility as a "threat" against a tenant for late rent or any other reason.

Special Circumstances for Utilities

Utilities, though, are tricky. There *are* cases where local utilities may hold property owners responsible for unpaid utilities in the form of a lien on the property. This depends on state and county law, so be aware of the rules in your area.

I also have had questions from tenants about what happens if a landlord is responsible for the utility and it gets shut off due to nonpayment.

Again, the answer varies depending on county and sometimes by city, but Connecticut's process is similar to many state laws.

"Energy and Utility Problems with Landlords," a document provided by ctlawhelp.org, details what happens.

~~~

A utility company cannot shut off your service if your landlord is responsible for the bill, unless the company mails you notice by regular mail 13 days before or by certified mail 7 days before its plan to shut off service. The notice must include:

- the date of the planned shutoff,
- phone number and address of the utility company and the PURA, and
- what you can do to avoid a shutoff.

Separate Meter: If your apartment or house has its own separate meter that only covers your utility use, the utility can require you to put service in your name. If you do this, they cannot charge you a security deposit, and you do not have to pay any of the back utility bills owed by your landlord.

Shared Meter: If your apartment or home has a shared (master) meter that covers more than your utility use, you have three possibilities:

1. If all tenants agree in writing, service can be put in everyone's names, with an agreed upon plan for dividing the bill and responsibility for payment. If at least one tenant is making his/her payment under this kind of plan, service cannot be shut

off. Any tenant or the utility can end this arrangement at any time, for any reason, by requesting in writing that it be ended.

2. You can get service in your name and only pay the part of the bill estimated to cover your service. The utility company can give you this estimate. The landlord is responsible for any portion of the bill that you did not pay because it was not for your utility service.

3. If you do not agree to either option above, or you agreed but then told the utility you wanted to end the arrangement, the utility cannot shut off your service. It can sue the landlord and ask the court to appoint a "receiver" who would collect rent and pay the utility bills.

Note: If you pay the utility company under any of the above options, you can deduct the full amount of your payments from your rent.

~~~

With this said, if you're a rental owner that resides in an area where the owner is ultimately responsible for a particular utility, you have two options.

1. Write the lease so that you pay the "said utility," but raise the rent by more than the average monthly cost of the utility. This is because if utilities are included in rent, they are often abused because the tenant doesn't see the bill.

So if rent is $500 and the utility usually costs $50, make the rent $575.

2. Write the lease so that the tenant is responsible for the "said utility," payable to you as additional rent each month, due with the next rent payment.

This means you leave the utility in your name and you get the bills. You copy the bills and send them to the tenant, who includes the amount with his next month's rent. It's a hassle, but the utility bill stays current.

If the tenant fails to pay the bill, write in the tenant's rent receipt that the utility was subtracted from the rent. Rent is now in arrears, and you now send the appropriate pay or quit notice.

If you want to know if a tenant has left a landlord holding utility bills in the past, visit www.realtenanthistory.com and check reviews and ratings from prior landlords.

17 – How to Lower Property Taxes (Indiana Example)

If there is one thing all Independent Rental Owners despise, it's property taxes. We have no control over them. It's always a surprise to open the letter each year and see the figure—and it's not the pleasant kind of surprise, either.

Property taxes aren't going away, though. We need to learn how property taxes are computed and what tools can help us reduce the annual amount.

The chart below shows what my property taxes were from 1997-2014. In 2001, my taxes increased 47%, shooting up from $8,313 to $12,219. Then in 2004, they increased by another 34%, jumping from $12,157 to $16,315.

I was dumbfounded by these increases. Nothing had changed with the actual properties.

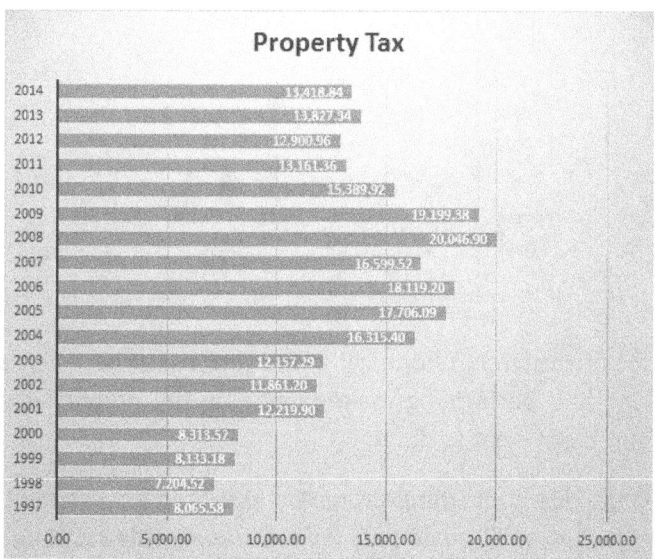

Both times I experienced a spike in taxes, I spoke with my county assessor, who said there wasn't anything I could do about the amount. But given the dramatic changes year after year, I decided to find a way to stabilize my property taxes so that I could at least budget for them. So I dug into research I should have done when I purchased my first rental property.

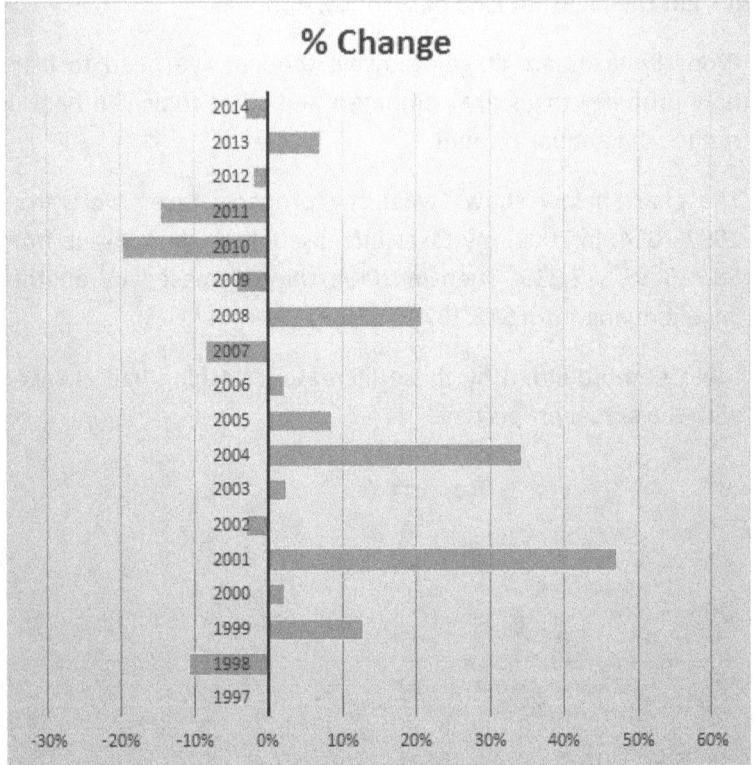

After a lot of research, phone calls, and letters, all between a fulltime job and performing maintenance on my properties, I finally figured out what to do.

The Indiana code concerning property taxes is in government-ese, as expected, so I'll share only the most applicable section.

Indiana Code - Section 6-1.1-4-39:

Assessment of rental property and mobile homes; low income rental housing exclusion

(a) For assessment dates after February 28, 2005, except as provided in subsections (c) and (e), the true tax value of real property regularly used to rent or otherwise furnish residential accommodations for periods of thirty (30) days or more and that has more than four (4) rental units is the lowest valuation determined by applying each of the following appraisal approaches:

[...]

(3) Income capitalization approach, using an applicable capitalization method and appropriate capitalization rates that are developed and used in computations that lead to an indication of value commensurate with the risks for the subject property use.

> (b) The gross rent multiplier method is the preferred method of valuing:
>
>> (1) real property that has at least one (1) and not more than four (4) rental units; and
>>
>> (2) mobile homes assessed under IC 6-1.1-7. (c) A township assessor (if any) or the county assessor is not required to appraise real property referred to in subsection

[...]

For the complete code, visit http://codes.lp.findlaw.com/incode/6/1.1/4/6-1.1-4-39#sthash.EBPJj4cV.dpuf

So what does all this mean?

The preferred method of assessing a rental property value in Indiana is using the gross rent multiplier (GRM). To make sense of that, I had to figure out how to compute the GRM.

The GRM is figured by dividing the market value of a property by the annual gross income generated by the property.

Here's an example. If a property sold for $750,000 and it brings in $110,000 a year in income, the GRM is 6.82. In other words:

Market Value / Annual Gross Income = GRM

$750,000 / $110,000 = 6.82

You can do the reverse. You can estimate the value of a property based on the GRM.

Let's say you did an analysis of recent comparable sold properties and found an average GRM of 6.75. If you know a property's gross income, say $68,000 annually, you can approximate the market value of the property.

GRM x Annual Gross Income = Market Value

6.75 x $68,000 = $459,000

If the property's listed for sale at $695,000, you probably don't want to waste time looking at it for purchase.

The assessor uses this equation to determine the market value of your rental property. Your task is to ensure the assessor is using the best and most accurate GRM and Annual Gross Income numbers.

Again, for Indiana, that means getting the county assessor the proper paperwork, which means sending

1. A completed Assessor's worksheet

2. Three+ years of Profit and Loss Statements for each property
3. Schedule E from your tax return, or Form 8825 if it is a corporation

Examples of each are shown on the following pages.

County Assessor Worksheet:

Kim Miller
Noble County Assessor
Courhouse - Room 100
101 N Orange Street - Albion IN 46701
Phone (260) 636-2297
Fax: (260) 636-3538

Landlord Income and Expense Data 4 Units or Less
Owner: Attainment, Inc.
Mailing Address: P.O. Box 563, Kendallville IN 46755
Phone #:   (260) 347-5835   Cell#:   (260) 226-0643
Tax/Parcel ID#:   008-100427-00

The Indiana General Assembly under IC 6-1.1-4-4.5 and the Indiana Dept. of Local Gov. under 50ICA 21 requires that assessing officials reassess certain rental property, by considering income and expense data. Reviewing this information could lower the assessed value of your property, resulting in a lower tax bill.

Property Address and Number of Units:
111 Kimball Avenue, Kendallville IN 46755

1. Is this Property Rented: Yes
2. How Many Rentalable Units: 1   Units
3. Gross Annual Rents:

	Yearly Gross Revenue			
Unit # 1	$ 525.00			
Unit # 2	$	-		
Unit # 3	$	-		
Unit # 4	$	-	Total All Units:	$ 525.00

5. Have You purchase this property in the last 3 years? (No)
6. If you purchased the property in the last 3 years: (N/A)
7. If you purchased the property in the last 3 years: (N/A)
8. If you purchase the porperty in the last 3 years: (N/A)
9. In order to quality fot he GRM you must provide to the asse
years of Income and Expense Statements (Schedule E)
    For # 9, See Attached documentation, and **(YES)** this
    was rented on March 1st of this year.

3+ Years of Profit and Loss

Attainment, Inc.
Profit & Loss Prev Year Comparison
2013, 2012, 2011, 2010, 2009, 2008, 2007, 2006
(908-100427-00)   01/14/2014

Ordinary Income/Expense	Jan - Dec 13	Jan - Dec 12	Jan - Dec 11	Jan - Dec 10	Jan - Dec 09	Jan - Dec 08	Jan - Dec 07	Jan - Dec 06	8 Year Avg	Monthly
Income										
Rental										
· Late Fees	0.00	0.00	0.00	0.00	200.00	100.00	0.00	0.00	42.86	3.57
Property 10 (111 Kimball)	7,085.46	5,515.00	6,654.25	6,975.00	7,200.00	7,199.88	2,400.00	5,818.00	6,147.08	512.26
Total Rental	7,085.46	5,515.00	6,654.25	6,975.00	7,400.00	7,299.88	2,400.00	5,818.00	6,189.94	515.83
Total Income	7,085.46	5,515.00	6,654.25	6,975.00	7,400.00	7,299.88	2,400.00	5,818.00	6,189.94	515.83
Gross Profit	7,085.46	5,515.00	6,654.25	6,975.00	7,400.00	7,299.88	2,400.00	5,818.00	6,189.94	515.83
Expense										
Depreciation Expense	1,599.84	1,599.84	1,599.84	1,599.84	1,599.84	1,599.84	1,599.84	1,599.84	1,599.84	133.32
Expensed Equipment	0.00	0.00	0.00	0.00	206.70	115.21	0.00	0.00	45.99	3.83
Insurance										
House Insurance	628.92	958.00	628.92	628.51	611.26	603.00	603.00	603.00	665.94	55.50
Total Insurance	628.92	958.00	628.92	628.51	611.26	603.00	603.00	603.00	665.94	55.50
Interest Expense										
Finance Charge	0.00	0.00	0.00	0.00	1,072.60	816.86	239.86	0.00	304.19	25.35
Loan Interest	1,058.40	1,435.00	1,421.99	1,468.49	774.47	874.61	1,176.60	1,606.00	1,172.79	97.73
Total Interest Expense	1,058.40	1,435.00	1,421.99	1,468.49	1,847.07	1,691.47	1,416.46	1,606.00	1,476.98	123.08
Repairs										
Building Repairs	1,120.00	279.00	2,701.07	0.00	2,594.00	0.00	0.00	4,288.91	956.30	79.69
Snow Removal	0.00	0.00	0.00	0.00	0.00	500.00	0.00	0.00	71.43	5.95
Total Repairs	1,120.00	279.00	2,701.07	0.00	2,594.00	500.00	0.00	4,288.91	1,027.72	85.64
Taxes										
Property	1,073.00	1,163.00	1,111.00	1,386.88	1,149.58	1,176.40	907.76	964.54	1,138.23	94.85
Total Taxes	1,073.00	1,163.00	1,111.00	1,386.88	1,149.58	1,176.40	907.76	964.54	1,138.23	94.85
Utilities										
Electric	0.00	-4.81	-13.13	15.12	21.17	-8.32	0.00	-16.50	1.43	0.12
Garbage Pickup	410.85	521.64	469.47	470.78	229.72	318.83	782.13	872.86	457.63	38.14
Gas	0.00	108.96	64.42	28.77	882.23	310.95	701.84	12.06	299.60	24.97
Water	0.00	0.00	120.00	0.00	0.00	0.00	0.00	0.00	17.14	1.43
Total Utilities	410.85	625.79	640.76	514.67	1,133.12	621.46	1,483.97	868.42	775.80	64.65
Total Expense	5,891.01	6,060.63	8,103.58	5,598.39	9,141.57	6,307.38	6,011.03	9,930.71	6,730.51	560.88
Net Ordinary Income	1,194.45	-545.63	-1,449.33	1,376.61	-1,741.57	992.50	-3,611.03	-4,112.71	-540.57	-45.05
Net Income	**1,194.45**	**-545.63**	**-1,449.33**	**1,376.61**	**-1,741.57**	**992.50**	**-3,611.03**	**-4,112.71**	**-540.57**	**-45.05**

And then the Schedule E, or Form **8825**.

Form 8825 (Rev December 2010) — Rental Real Estate Income and Expenses of a Partnership or an S Corporation
Department of the Treasury, Internal Revenue Service
► See instructions. ► Attach to Form 1065, Form 1065-B, or Form 1120S.
OMB No. 1545-1186

Name: Attainment, Inc.

1. Show the type and address of each property. For each rental real estate property listed, report the number of days rented at fair rental value and days with personal use. See instructions. See page 2 to list additional properties.

	Physical address of each property — street, city, state, ZIP code	Type — Enter code 1-8; see page 2 for list	Fair Rental Days	Personal Use Days
A	116 N. Park Avenue, Kendallville, IN 46755	2	15,299	0
B	1004 S. Garden St, Kendallville, IN 46755	2	18,498	0
C	212 E. Wayne St, Kendallville, IN 46755	2	8,671	0
D	217 E. Wayne Street, Kendallville, IN 46755	2	5,790	0

Rental Real Estate Income		Properties A	B	C	D
2 Gross rents	2	15,299	18,123	8,671	5,790
Rental Real Estate Expenses					
3 Advertising	3				
4 Auto and travel	4				
5 Cleaning and maintenance	5				
6 Commissions	6				
7 Insurance	7	796	672	465	465
8 Legal and other professional fees	8	1,000	1,000	1,000	1,000
9 Interest	9	5,740	5,740	2,870	2,870
10 Repairs	10	1,176	6,499	40	40
11 Taxes	11	1,637	2,614	709	383
12 Utilities	12	1,443	1,666	977	1,418
13 Wages and salaries	13				
14 Depreciation (see instructions)	14	1,522	3,091	1,986	1,986
15 Other (list)	15				
16 Total expenses for each property. Add lines 3 through 15	16	13,314	21,282	8,047	8,162
17 Income or (Loss) from each property. Subtract line 16 from line 2	17	1,985	-3,159	624	

18a Total gross rents. Add gross rents from line 2, columns A through H
18b Total expenses. Add total expenses from line 16, columns A through H
19 Net gain (loss) from Form 4797, Part II, line 17, from the disposition of property from rental real estate activities.
20a Net income (loss) from rental real estate activities from partnerships, estates, and trusts in which this partnership or S corporation is a partner or beneficiary (from Schedule K-1).
b Identify below the partnerships, estates, or trusts from which net income (loss) is shown on line 20a. Attach a schedule if more space is needed:
(1) Name (2) Employer Identification number

21 Net rental real estate income (loss). Combine lines 18a through 20a. Enter the result here and on:
* Form 1065 or 1120S: Schedule K, line 2, or
* Form 1065-B: Part I, line 4

BAA For Paperwork Reduction Act Notice, see the separate instructions.

Form 8825 (12-2010) Attainment, Inc. Page 2

1. Show the type and address of each property. For each rental real estate property listed, report the number of days at fair rental value and days with personal use. See instructions.

Physical address of each property — street, city, state, ZIP code	Type — Enter code 1-8: see below for list	Fair Rental Days	Personal Use Days
E 219 E Wayne St, Kendallville, IN 46755	2	11,400	0
F 224 E Wayne St, Kendallville, IN 46755	1	8,340	0
G 121 N Orchard St, Kendallville, IN 46755	2	9,855	0
H 513 E Mitchell St, Kendallville, IN 46755	2	9,770	0

		Properties		
Rental Real Estate Income	E	F	G	H
2 Gross rents	11,400	8,340	9,855	9,770
Rental Real Estate Expenses				
3 Advertising				157
4 Auto and travel				
5 Cleaning and maintenance				
6 Commissions				
7 Insurance	1,070	539	617	721
8 Legal and other professional fees	1,000	1,000	1,000	1,000
9 Interest	5,740	1,435	2,870	2,870
10 Repairs	1,695	40	667	4,007
11 Taxes	1,641	1,075	1,219	1,103
12 Utilities	1,504	374	759	1,101
13 Wages and salaries				
14 Depreciation (see instructions)	3,853	981	1,986	1,549
15 Other (list)				
16 Total expenses for each property. Add lines 3 through 15	16,503	5,444	9,118	12,508
17 Income or (Loss) from each property. Subtract line 16 from line 2	-5,103	2,896	737	-2,738

Allowable Codes for Type of Property
1— Single Family Residence
2— Multi-Family Residence
3— Vacation or Short-term Rental
4— Commercial
5— Land
6— Royalties
7— Self-Rental
8— Other (include description with the code on Form 8825 or on a separate statement)

BAA

Form 8825 (12-2010) Attainment, Inc.

1. Show the type and address of each property. For each rental real estate property listed, report the number of days at fair rental value and days with personal use. See instructions.

Physical address of each property — street, city, state, ZIP code	Type — Enter code 1-8; see below for list	Fair Rental Days	Personal Use Days
E 521 E Mitchell St, Kendallville, IN 46755	2	13,475	0
F 111 Kimball Avenue, Kendallville, IN 46755	1	6,515	0
G			
H			

Rental Real Estate Income		Properties			
		E	F	G	H
2 Gross rents	2	13,475.	6,515.		
Rental Real Estate Expenses					
3 Advertising	3				
4 Auto and travel	4				
5 Cleaning and maintenance	5				
6 Commissions	6				
7 Insurance	7	697.	958.		
8 Legal and other professional fees	8	1,000.	1,000.		
9 Interest	9	4,305.	1,435.		
10 Repairs	10	1,151.	279.		
11 Taxes	11	1,617.	1,163.		
12 Utilities	12	2,791.	626.		
13 Wages and salaries	13				
14 Depreciation (see instructions)	14	2,323.	1,600.		
15 Other (list) ▶					
	15				
16 Total expenses for each property. Add lines 3 through 15	16	13,884.	7,061.		
17 Income or (Loss) from each property. Subtract line 16 from line 2	17	-409.	-546.		

Allowable Codes for Type of Property
1— Single Family Residence
2— Multi-Family Residence
3— Vacation or Short-term Rental
4— Commercial
5— Land
6— Royalties
7— Self-Rental
8— Other (include description with the code on Form 8825 or on a separate statement)

BAA

These forms need to be sent for *every property*. Over the past 12 years, I averaged about 10 hours a year working on the necessary forms.

Doing this right is not a quick process, and it involves more than just filling out the forms and sending them to the county assessor.

Every April, I send in the required forms. In early May, I call the assessor to make sure he received my forms. During the summer, the assessor does his processing and sends out the results in September or October.

When I receive the results, I call the assessor's office to voice my concerns on the results. It usually takes two or three calls before I manage to speak to the right person.

Once I'm content with the assessed values, I stop the calls to the assessor's office. The squeaky wheel has gotten the grease.

If you return to the graphs at the beginning of this chapter, you can see I began Operation Squeaky Wheel in 2004. My taxes in 2005 and 2006 still went up, but not as sharply. In 2007, they went down.

In 2008, a new assessor was elected, so I had to start Operation Squeaky Wheel from the top. You have to love politics.

As of 2014, my effective property taxes are at 2001 levels, even without taking account of inflation. All it took was a lot of time, effort, research, and persistence.

Lesson: In the rental business, one of your biggest costs is property taxes. It's worth the effort to know the laws and fight for your rights. The last thing an elected person wants is an unhappy constituent. Be persistent.

18 – Mower Boy

In 2002, a friend of mine named Bill became unemployed just before summer started. Since he knew I owned apartments, he asked if there was any upkeep work he could do for me.

My first thought was, *Hey, I won't have to mow this summer! Bill can do it.*

"How about you mow all my properties?" I asked.

"Sure. I can do that."

Mowing was now off my To Do List for the summer.

There were 11 properties that each needed mowed once a week. Mowing entailed more than simply pushing a mower around the yard. Bill also needed to trim the bushes, trim the grass, and use a blower to clean off all the sidewalks. He also needed to spray the parking areas for weeds every other week.

Little did I know that all this landscaping work would be about more than keeping the lawns looking nice.

Right before I hired him to do all the lawn care, I rented a three-bedroom apartment to three single girls. They loved the apartment. It was relatively secluded. The back porch roof couldn't be seen from the street or by any of the neighbors.

This is the spot they picked for sunbathing.

Well, Bill stopped by that apartment about every three days to mow, trim, rake, and do whatever could possibly be done. Not only did he enjoy the view, but the apartment now had one of the finest manicured lawns I'd seen that summer. Luckily, he was not charging me for these "special" visits.

While Bill enjoyed the view from that lawn, it seemed a tenant from another apartment enjoyed the view of *him*.

The first time Bill mowed this property, he noticed the tenant watched him from the window—the whole time.

He didn't think much of it, but it happened the second week, too. That's when he first mentioned it to me.

This happened every week for about a month until one day the tenant left her window. And came outside. Scantily clad.

"Hey, Mower Boy, you want to come inside and earn a few bucks?"

Bill pretended not to hear. He didn't know how to respond, so he just kept mowing. When he returned home, he called me up and told me what happened.

I guess the tables had turned.

This happened the next two weeks as well. I finally had to stop by the apartment to talk to the tenant about her comments to Bill.

It wasn't the easiest thing to bring up, but I managed and she confessed that she had said such things. "I'm sorry. I'm just lonely and I was looking for a good time."

I asked her not to do it again. She didn't. That was the end of it.

This situation is a reminder of one of the most valuable lessons I shared in Volume 1 of *80/20 Landlording*—Don't be caught alone with a tenant. This can take some planning, but it's well worth the effort.

19 – The Bachelor Pad

In the winter of 1997. I put an ad in the local paper. (This was back when people actually read the newspaper and looked at the ads.) I had an empty efficiency apartment. It was partly furnished and rent was only $300 monthly. Tenants paid electric and I paid all other utilities.

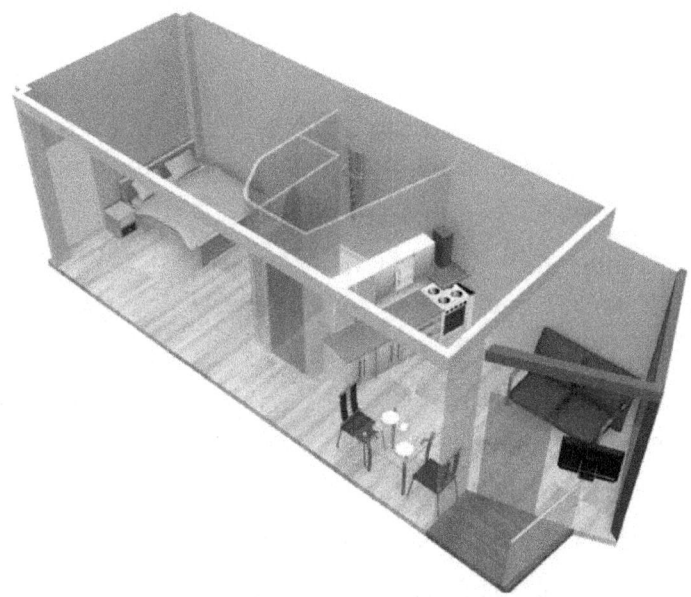

After receiving a few calls, I set up a Saturday to show the apartment, making sure to schedule the interested parties about 20 minutes apart from each other.

One particular gentleman caught my attention. I'll call him Ted. He showed up in a nice car. I showed him the apartment then had him fill out an application. "It'll be hard to verify my employment," he said. "I'm self-employed and own a restaurant about 15 miles north of here." It was on a lake in the area.

"I'll still run my normal checks. I'll get back to you after that." As it happened, I ended up renting to Ted the next week.

Most of my tenants feel comfortable calling me to let me know what's going on at the properties. Another of my tenants, we'll call him Robert, kept me posted with weekly updates.

Robert knew I'd rented the efficiency apartment, but he hadn't seen anything being moved in yet—and he told me so.

I called Ted. "Is everything going fine?" I asked.

"Yes. I'm still waiting on some of the furniture I ordered. That's why I haven't moved much in yet."

Robert's next report indicated that he'd seen a bed, table, and chairs transferred to the unit. "He's finally getting moved in," Robert said.

Ted rented the apartment from February 1997 to February 1999. Robert lived on the same property in a one-bedroom apartment this entire time.

During these two years, Robert was amazed at how many different women entered Ted's apartment, with and without him.

It turns out this was Ted's Bachelor Pad.

Based on Robert's many reports, Ted spent only four or five nights a month at the apartment, though he visited during the day more often. From time to time, one of his many girlfriends did spend nights at the apartment.

It was late 1998 when I first received a call from a woman asking lots of questions about Ted. She wanted to know where he was renting.

I did not share the location of his apartment, but I did let her know we had a tenant named Ted.

"I need the address," she demanded angrily. "Give it to me."

I did not.

She called several times over the next month, asking the same question. "What's the address?"

"I can't share that information with you. I'm sorry."

Then, one day, I received a phone call from Robert. "There's a woman knocking on all the doors asking for Ted." She had finally discovered the property at which Ted rented his apartment.

Since she was disturbing the other tenants, I decided to drive over and see what she needed.

When I confronted her, I learned the truth. She was Ted's wife. "I know he has a place he takes his girlfriends," she said. "Let me into his apartment."

"I can't. Your name isn't on the lease."

"I'll call the police if you won't let me in."

I let her do so. The police came and told her exactly what I had told her. She wasn't on the lease, so she didn't have the right to forcibly enter the unit.

"Will you please inform her she's not allowed on the property anymore?" I asked the police. They did so, explaining that if she was found on the property again, she would be arrested for trespassing.

I never heard from her again. And—surprise, surprise!—Ted left the apartment the next month.

His cover was blown. The apartment would no longer work as his Bachelor Pad.

20 – Men in Black

In February 2001, I setup an appointment to show an apartment to a gentleman named Ahmed Humaidi. He seemed like a nice guy. He worked at a local factory. Everything on his application checked out great. He did say he had a friend who would be living with him whose name he did not want on the lease, but I didn't have any problems with that.

On March 1st, 2001, I rented to him. He moved in that day with his friend. Over the next few months, I stopped by to check in a couple times. Everything seemed to be going well.

"I'll have two more friends moving in. They want to save money to get their own apartments," he told me.

"That's fine, as long as no other people move in."

There were now four people in a two-bedroom apartment. The rent was $400 a month, so they were splitting it $100 each.

March, April, and May went by without issue. In June, I received a call from a neighbor who said the front picture window was broken, so I stopped by the apartment. Ahmed answered the door.

"One of my friends fell into the window," he explained. "That's how it broke."

"You should have called me. Do you know this will cost $500 to fix?" I was a little pissed.

Ahmed reached into his wallet and pulled out five $100 bills.

"I'll have it fixed by the end of the day," I told him.

I didn't hear anything from him or his neighbors until September 10th, 2001. "He has a bunch of friends over," his neighbor complained to me that day, "and they're making a lot of noise on the front porch."

It was about 9 pm, so I didn't go over to the apartment that evening.

I had to work the next day, September 11th, so I wasn't able to stop by the apartment that morning to find out what had been going on the night before.

Other things ended up taking my attention that day.

I spent most of the day watching the news at work, and when I got home I immediately turned the news on. I forgot about the tenants making noise.

The next day, I finally stopped by the apartment. While I was walking to the door, the neighbor who had complained yelled out to me that Ahmed and his friends had moved out the night before.

"I saw them with suitcases, bedding, and some kitchen things," he said. "They packed their car and drove off."

That was a little odd.

I knocked on the door. No answer. I let myself in. I hadn't been in the apartment since Ahmed had moved in. I found a TV in the living room, four mattresses (two in each bedroom), a few items in the kitchen, three posters, and nothing else.

I decided to call their employer. They all worked for the same factory.

"They haven't been to work since Monday," she said. That had been September 10th.

They had had a party on the 10th, then moved out on the 11th. I couldn't get over the timing. I didn't do anything with the apartment for two weeks.

When I did return to the apartment, I checked to see if they had been collecting their mail. They hadn't. The mailbox was full. Inside was a bunch of junk mail and a bank statement.

I pitched everything but the bank statement. I opened it. I knew I shouldn't have, but I couldn't help it. The balance on the account was more than $450,000. From their most recent transactions, I saw they had moved to the Detroit area.

I called the FBI.

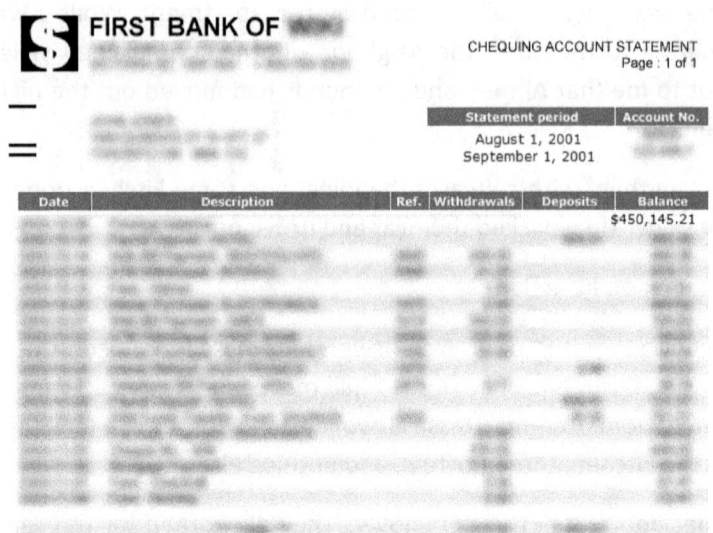

As Paul Harvey would say, "And now the rest of the story!"

"Don't touch anything in the unit," the FBI told me. "Don't do anything with the apartment until we inspect it."

The next day, two FBI agents stopped at my house, and I directed them to the rental unit.

Since there wasn't a lot of furniture or other belongings, it didn't take them long to inspect the property. They removed the posters on the wall. Behind one of the posters were five calling cards with phone numbers written on them. They took the calling cards and all the mail, including the bank statements.

I then went through a two-hour interview with the agents. I told them everything I knew about the tenants. I gave them copies of Ahmed's application and lease.

When they heard that I had received a call from the neighbor on September 10th, they interviewed the neighbor as well. He gave them an animated story about what he believed the group was partying about.

"They kept chanting, 'Death to America! Death to America!'" he told them.

I asked the agents for their business cards so if anything else showed up, I could send it to them.

Over the next two months, additional bank statements arrived. I did not open these but forwarded them to the FBI agents.

After a couple months, and once new tenants were in the unit, the mail stopped coming for the prior tenants.

I never heard anything more from the FBI.

Appendix 1 – Indiana Eviction Process

This guide is for informational purposes only and should not be relied on for legal advice. If you need legal advice, contact an attorney.

This guide presents an overview of rules and procedures for the eviction process. The specific rules and procedures in your court may vary from those presented here. Check with your court about local rules.

What is an eviction?

An eviction is when your landlord makes you move out of your home, usually by getting an order from a court, but not always.

Does my landlord have to take me to court to evict me?

The landlord should take you to court. Most landlords will file a case in court to evict you. Some landlords, however, may just try to lock you out of the home. Landlords are not supposed to do this, but some do try. If your landlord threatens to change your locks to get you out of the home, you should try to keep someone in the home at all times and call the police if the landlord tries to change the locks.

My landlord has told me I must leave the apartment by the end of the week. What should I do?

First, do not panic if the landlord says you must leave by a certain day. You do not have to leave until there is an order from the court saying you must leave. Landlords can't evict tenants without first going to court and getting an order. Also, landlords cannot change the locks, cut off the utilities, or do other things to try to get you leave.

Generally, landlords can evict you before your lease is up only if you have broken your lease. Common reasons for eviction include the tenant hasn't paid rent or has damaged the property.

You should try to talk to the landlord and see if you can work something out with the landlord to see if the landlord will agree you can stay. If you agree you have broken your lease because you owe money, maybe you can work out an agreement with the landlord to pay what you owe. If you do make an agreement with the landlord, make sure you get it in writing.

Can my landlord lock me out of my home?

No, your landlord usually cannot lock you out. As long as you haven't abandoned your home, your landlord cannot change the locks, install a deadbolt, take off doors, or do anything to stop you from entering your home. (However, your landlord CAN do these things if he has a court order that says he can).

The only exception to this rule is if you have not paid or offered to pay your rent AND your home has been abandoned. If it looks like you don't live there anymore (for example, your things are gone and you have not been there for awhile), the home may be considered abandoned.

Can my landlord shut off my utilities if I haven't paid my rent?

No, not unless your landlord has a court order allowing him to shut off your utilities, or you have abandoned your home. (However, the landlord may be able to shut off your utilities if there is an emergency, to make repairs, or for necessary construction). Keep in mind that the landlord does not have to pay for the utilities, unless the landlord has agreed to do so.

Can my landlord take my things out of my home, or stop me from getting my things, if I don't pay my rent?

No, generally your landlord cannot take your things or stop you from getting your things even if you did not pay your rent.

There are exceptions to this rule. Your landlord may be able to take your things or stop you from getting your things if:

- Your landlord has a court order that allows him to take or sell your things; or
- You sign an agreement with your landlord, separate from your lease, that your landlord may hold your things in exchange for the landlord not evicting you.

Even if the landlord has a court order that allows him to take your property, you can get certain things known as "exempt" items returned to you immediately without paying any money. You can always get:

- medically necessary items;
- items used in your business;
- a week's supply of clothing for household members;
- blankets; and
- things needed for school.

What can I do if my landlord has wrongfully locked me out of my apartment, shut off my utilities, or taken my things?

You need to get an EMERGENCY ORDER. The best way to get one is to talk to an attorney who can help you. You can also go to your local small claims court for an emergency order. The emergency order can tell your landlord to let you back in your home, turn on your utilities, or give your things back to you.

To get an emergency order, you must file a sworn written statement with the court. In a sworn statement, you promise everything in it is true. You need to tell the court exactly what your landlord has done, or threatened to do, and what problems you are having because of your landlord's actions. Include any costs you have had to pay because of your landlord's actions (such as hotel bills). When you ask for an emergency order, the court must set an emergency hearing within 3 business days.

What will happen at the emergency hearing?

The court can allow you back into your home and/or order the landlord to give your things back if you prove that:

- Your landlord threatened to lock you out or did lock you out, (or removed the doors or windows or shut off your utilities); AND
- You will suffer immediate and serious damage.

Can my landlord get an emergency order, too?

Yes. Your landlord can get an emergency order if he proves that you have committed or threatened to commit waste (damages) to your home, and that he has suffered immediate and serious damages because of your actions. Waste does NOT include failing to pay your rent. Your landlord can get an emergency order that tells you to:

- move from your home; or
- stop committing damage to your home.

My landlord got an emergency order evicting me, but I didn't know about the hearing. Is there anything that I can do?

When a landlord asks for an emergency hearing and order, the court clerk must give you notice of the date, time and place of the hearing. If you don't get notice of the hearing, you can ask the court to set aside the emergency order, and give you a new hearing. If this happens to you, you should contact a private attorney or your local legal services office. If you are unable to get an attorney, you can file a motion with the court yourself.

What if my landlord has told me he is going to change the locks, but he hasn't done it yet?

You should contact an attorney if your landlord is threatening to lock you out. If possible, you should try to keep someone in your home at all times. If the landlord then tries to change the locks, you can call the police. You may want to keep very important papers or other possessions with you or at a friend or relative's home in case the landlord does change the locks. You should be able to get your items back from a landlord who has wrongfully locked you out, but that can take awhile.

What if my landlord wants to evict me and I don't think I have violated any terms of my lease?

If possible, try to talk to the landlord. If you don't think you have violated your lease, you can wait and see if the landlord files an eviction case in court. If the landlord files an eviction case, you will have to go to court. The landlord will have to prove you violated the lease, and you will get a chance to tell your side of the story. If your landlord has threatened to evict you, you may want to start gathering evidence (such as receipts, etc.) to give to the court to show you have not violated your lease.

What happens if the landlord files an eviction?

Here are the general steps in an eviction:

1. The landlord tells the tenant the landlord wants the tenant to move out.
2. The landlord files a case against the tenant.
3. The tenant receives notice of the lawsuit by certified mail or by the Sheriff.
4. The first hearing is to decide who has the right to possession of the apartment. If the tenant is in violation of the contract (for example, if the tenant is behind in rent), the landlord will have the right to possession and the court will order that the tenant be out by a certain date. (This is usually within a few days of the court hearing; you don't get much time to move). If the court finds the tenant hasn't violated the lease, then the case is over and the tenant does not have to move.
5. There is often a second hearing for the court to decide if the tenant owes the landlord any money. The tenant

can also tell the court if the tenant thinks the landlord owes the tenant any money.

Do I need an attorney to represent me?

An attorney might be able to help you in court or help you negotiate an agreement with your landlord. If you cannot afford to hire an attorney, you could apply for legal services at your local legal services program.

If you don't have an attorney, you should still go to court on your own. Most evictions are in small claims court. In small claims court, people often do not have an attorney. The judge will let you tell your side of the story.

What if I am behind in my rent?

If you are behind in your rent and the landlord files an eviction case in court, you will be evicted. There is really no defense for not paying the rent. So, if you lost your job and cannot pay your rent, it is better to try to work out a payment plan with the landlord before you go to court – and, like always, put it in writing.

If you cannot work out anything with the landlord, you should start thinking about where you will move. The courts will generally give tenants only a few days to move out after an eviction hearing.

I am behind in rent; should I just move out?

If you can't work a deal out with your landlord, you may want to go ahead and move if you have someplace to go. If you know you have violated your lease, you may want to avoid going to court. (If you have an eviction on your record, it might be harder for you to find a new place to rent). Maybe your landlord will agree to let you stay a little longer if you agree to move out by a certain date, and if you can pay some rent money. Get any agreement with your landlord in writing.

If you don't have any other place to go, you can just stay in the home until you go to court and the court says you must move.

What if I live in subsidized housing?

If you live in subsidized housing (where the government pays part of your rent), you may have special rights and the landlord might have special rules to follow.

You should definitely contact an attorney if your landlord is threatening to evict you from subsidized housing. If you are evicted from subsidized housing, you may not be able to get into other subsidized housing.

What should I do when I move out of the housing?

Many times tenants lose their security deposits and even have to pay more money after they move out because of damage done to the apartment. When you move out, the landlord will compare the condition of the apartment with its condition when you moved in. If you have damaged the apartment, you will have to pay for the costs of repairing those damages. But there is a difference between normal use and "damage." For example, stains on the carpet is damage, but dirty carpet on the traffic areas is normal use.

The landlord has 45 days to either return your security deposit or send you a letter telling you what damages you are being charged for. If the landlord does not do this, the landlord cannot charge you for any damages. BUT, you must tell the landlord in writing of your new address. You should keep a copy of this letter.

When leaving the apartment, you should:

- Leave it clean
- Tell the landlord in writing of your new address and keep a copy of the letter.
- Return all the keys.
- Do an inspection with the landlord.
- Take pictures or a video of the apartment so that you can have it as proof of the condition when you left.

What else should I do to protect myself?

- Save all documentation and letters you receive or write about the apartment. Save copies of everything.
- Put in writing all "side deals" or agreements outside the original contract.
- Know the terms of the lease.
- Attend all hearings to defend your rights.

What if the court has told me to move, but I don't move?

If the court has ordered you to move out and you don't move out, the court will send someone (such as the sheriff or local constable) to the home to move your belongings out for you. Your belongings will usually be put in storage, and then you will need to pay for the moving and the storage.

If the court has told you to move, you should make every effort to move out. You should make sure you have your important belongings out of the home.

The court said I have to move, but I don't agree. What can I do?

If the court has issued an order that says you have to move, you don't have many options. You can appeal the trial court's decision to the next level of courts (which is usually the Indiana Court of Appeals). Appealing to the Indiana Court of Appeals is difficult and you should talk to an attorney about this option.

In some counties (such as Marion County), you can appeal the Small Claims Court decision to the county's Superior Court. This is not as difficult as appealing to the Indiana Court of Appeals, but you should still talk to an attorney about this.

There are strict time limits for filing an appeal. If you think you might want to appeal a trial court's decision, you should contact an attorney right away.

Appendix 2 – Eviction Process Ohio

This guide is for informational purposes only and should not be relied on for legal advice. If you need legal advice, contact an attorney.

This guide presents an overview of rules and procedures for the eviction process. The specific rules and procedures in your court may vary from those presented here. Check with your court about local rules.

How does the eviction process start?

All evictions in Ohio must begin with a "Notice to Leave Premises," (commonly referred to as a three-day (3-day) notice).

Note that some notices may contain extra language if you live in housing built and/or subsidized by the government.

Can my landlord then come over and throw out all my belongings?

No, your landlord must wait three (3) days and then file an eviction action with the local court.

How will I know if my landlord files in court?

The court will deliver to you a copy of the complaint the landlord filed along with a summons prepared by the court to tell you what to do.

Read both the summons and complaint carefully.

Can I get a lawyer to represent me?

Perhaps.

How will I get the court papers?

You should get two (2) copies:

One (1) by regular mail

One (1) by certified mail, personal (hand delivered) service, or by leaving it at the residence.

How will I know when to go to court?

Read the summons carefully, since that information will be somewhere on the summons, but each court system prepares their own summons differently.

Should I go to court?

Yes, even if you move. If you think your landlord is wrong and should not be allowed to evict you, this is your chance to convince the court your landlord is wrong. Be prepared because you may not get another chance.

Why should I go if I have moved?

Tell the court you have moved, returned the keys to your landlord, have removed all the possessions you intended to take with you, and that you will not return. The court should dismiss the eviction claim if you have already given possession back to the landlord.

DO NOT ASSUME THAT YOUR LANDLORD WILL DO THIS FOR YOU, THEREFORE BELIEVING THAT IT IS NOT NECESSARY FOR YOU TO GO TO COURT.

Will I have much time to prepare for my case?

No, like most states, Ohio has an expedited eviction process. In Ohio, each county is permitted to create their own schedule for evictions; however, Ohio eviction law does require that you get the court papers at least seven (7) days before your court date.

If you receive your court papers less than seven (7) days before your court date, tell the court and you should set a continuance.

Can I bring letters and/or receipts with me to court?

Yes, and you should do so if they help explain your story. Keep in mind that letters from people who speak up in your behalf may be disallowed by the court as "hearsay."

Does this mean I should bring witnesses with me to court instead of letters written by them?

Yes. This is always the best way to make sure that what they have to say can be heard by the court.

What should I do when I go to court?

First and foremost — be on time! If you are late and your case has already been heard, you probably will not get another chance unless you have an extremely compelling reason.

Second, let someone from the court know you are there (typically the judge or magistrate will have a bailiff to assist them and call cases).

Third, sit in the courtroom to listen for your case to be called and be ready to tell the court your story when called.

Can I get a lawyer?

Yes, you may pay a lawyer to represent you. You may be expected to pay the referral lawyer and their rates vary greatly.

What if I can't afford a lawyer?

Contact your local legal aid program to see if they can assist you. Although legal aid is free, not every person is entitled to a lawyer. There are simply far more people contacting legal aid for help than there are lawyers available to represent all.

However, even if your local legal aid is unable to represent you, they may be able to provide with written information and/or general advice at a clinic that may help you prepare for your day in court.

Appendix 3 – Michigan Eviction Process

This guide is for informational purposes only and should not be relied on for legal advice. If you need legal advice, contact an attorney.

This guide presents an overview of rules and procedures for the eviction process. The specific rules and procedures in your court may vary from those presented here. Check with your court about local rules.

Landlord and Tenant Rights and Resources

If you are renting a home, apartment, mobile home or mobile home lot, or some other building from someone, you are a tenant. A landlord is the person who is renting the home, apartment, mobile home or mobile home lot, or some other building to you. A landlord is usually the property owner but not always. For example, sometimes the landlord is a person who is subleasing the property. Both the tenant and the landlord have legal rights. See general information about the resources and rights available in Tenant and Landlords, published by the Michigan Legislature. Other resources about landlord-tenant matters and relations are available from MichiganLegalAid.org, the Michigan State University College of Law Housing Clinic, and the University of Detroit Mercy School of Law.

If you want information about the mortgage foreclosure process, you may visit the website of the Michigan Foreclosure Prevention Project. If you are having difficulty with your mortgage, you may contact a Michigan State Housing Development Authority (MSHDA) certified nonprofit housing counselor. To find a counselor, go to http://www.mshda.info/counseling_search/, or contact MSHDA at 866-846-7432.

Reasons for Evicting a Tenant or Trespasser

A tenant or trespasser can be evicted from a property for several reasons. The most common reasons are:

- nonpayment of rent
- termination of periodic (month-to-month) tenancy or no-lease tenancy
- termination for lease violations (if the lease authorizes termination in these instances)

- expiration of the lease,
- serious and continuing health hazard on the rental property
- extensive and continuing damage to the rental property
- illegal drug activity or use on the rental property
- trespass onto or forcible retention of real property
- expiration of the redemption period following a mortgage foreclosure.

How to Evict a Tenant

A tenant cannot be evicted without a court order. The legal process for getting a court order requires:

Notice to the tenant, formal written complaint filed with the court, opportunity to answer and appear at a hearing/trial on the complaint, opportunity to demand a jury trial, entry of judgment of possession, and application and an order to evict.

Notice

In most situations, before a landlord can file a complaint with the court to evict a tenant, the tenant must be served with a written "notice to quit," "demand for possession," or some other written notice from a landlord. The notice may ask the tenant to pay rent, repair property, remove a health hazard, move out, or take some other action.

Complaint

If a notice to quit or demand for possession is required and after the specified time on the notice to quit or demand for possession has passed, the landlord (plaintiff) may file a complaint in the district court. Except for certain courts that have adopted a local court rule (listed below), a hearing (trial) will be scheduled by the clerk of the court and a summons (notice to appear in court) will be issued and served on the tenant (defendant).

Answer, Demand for Jury Trial, Hearing (Trial)

The defendant must appear and answer the complaint by the date on the summons. Appearance may be made by filing a written answer with the court and serving a copy on the landlord or by orally answering the allegations in the complaint at the hearing. Pursuant to local court rule, the following courts require a written response to be filed with the court before the hearing/trial will be scheduled: 1st District Court (Monroe County), 2A District Court (Lenawee County), 12th District Court (Jackson County), 18th District Court (City of Westland), 81st District Court (Alcona, Arenac, Iosco, and Oscoda Counties), 82nd District Court (Ogemaw County), and 95B District Court (Dickinson and Iron Counties).

The defendant can demand a jury trial in the first response to the complaint, whether written or oral. If a jury trial is demanded, the court will adjourn the trial. The court may also require the tenant to deposit future rent payments into an escrow account until the case is settled.

When the defendant appears, the court may hear/try the action, or adjourn the matter to a later date. At trial, the court must determine if there is an issue that can be "tried," and if not, it must enter a judgment.

Entry of Judgment

At the hearing (trial), the judge or jury will decide if and under what conditions the landlord should be given possession of the property. If the tenant fails to appear and answer the complaint, a default judgment giving the landlord possession of the property may be entered.

Application and Order of Eviction

Unless the court enters an immediate order of eviction, ten days after a judgment for possession has been entered a plaintiff may apply for an order to evict the tenant. This order authorizes a court officer, sheriff, police officer, or other person authorized by court rule to restore the plaintiff to peaceful possession of the property, which includes evicting the defendant and removing the defendant's belongings from the rental property.

How to Begin Eviction Proceedings for Nonpayment of Rent

If you are a landlord and the tenant has failed to pay rent, you may begin eviction proceedings by giving the tenant 7 days' notice to either pay the rent or move out or vacate the premises.

If the tenant does not pay the rent or move out within the time frame in the notice, you can file a complaint with the district court requesting the court to order eviction and to give you a judgment for damages, if any.

If you don't want to offer the tenant the option to pay the rent and simply want to evict the tenant and/or obtain a judgment to collect damages owed to you by the tenant, you must proceed on a different reason for eviction. This usually requires a notice to quit or demand for possession.

You can prepare your own notice or use the SCAO-approved form, Demand for Possession, Nonpayment or Rent (form DC 100a). If you prepare your own notice, it must comply with MCL 600.5716.

Giving Notice to a Tenant

The demand for possession must be served on the tenant. The demand may be served in one of three ways:

- by delivering it personally to the tenant;
- by delivering it on the premises to a member of the tenant's family or household, or an employee of the tenant, who is of suitable age and discretion, with a request that it be delivered to the tenant;
- by sending it by first-class mail addressed to the tenant.

Some examples of improper service are slipping the demand under the tenant's door, leaving the demand outside the tenant's door, attaching the demand to the property, or mailing the demand by methods that require a signature.

If the demand is mailed, the date of service is the next regular day for delivery of mail after the day it was mailed. When figuring out the date you want the tenant to move out by and when you can file a complaint, do not include days that mail is not delivered, such as Sundays and holidays. See general information about service.

What if You Get a Demand for Possession from a Landlord

If you are served with a demand for possession because of nonpayment of rent (this may be an SCAO-approved form called a Demand for Possession, Nonpayment of Rent, DC 100a) and you do in fact owe the rent, you may respond to the request in the demand by paying the rent or moving out or vacating the premises. If you disagree with the demand, you may want to contact an attorney (legal aid may be available in your area) or you may contact your landlord to attempt to resolve the problem.

Filing a Complaint Against a Tenant for Nonpayment of Rent

If you served a demand for possession because of nonpayment of rent and the tenant did not pay the rent or move out or vacate the premises as you requested in the demand, you may file a complaint with the district court to regain possession of your rental property and, if applicable, to get a judgment for money damages against the tenant. In certain circumstances it may not be necessary to file a complaint to regain possession of the property. Consult an attorney. See also MCL 600.2918(3) for details.

When you file a lawsuit against a tenant, you (the landlord) are called the plaintiff and the tenant is called the defendant. The plaintiff is usually the owner of the property, but not always. For example, the plaintiff can be someone who is subleasing the property. A paper copy of the complaint form is available from the court or you can complete it online (Complaint, Nonpayment of Rent, Landlord-Tenant, DC 102a).

The complaint must be filed with the district court where the property is located. A copy of the complaint and a notice of the court hearing must be served on the tenant. You can file your complaint with the court in person or by first-class mail. More detailed instructions for filing and serving the complaint are provided in the form packet (DC 102a).

There is a fee for filing a complaint against a tenant who has not paid rent. The cost of filing your lawsuit with the district court is $45.00. If you are seeking money damages, you must pay an additional filing fee as follows:

- $25 for damage claims up to $600
- $45 for damage claims from $600 to $1,750
- $65 for damage claims over $1,750 to $10,000
- $150 for damage claims over $10,000 to $25,000

The plaintiff (landlord) is responsible for paying the filing fee and other fees. If the judge rules in favor of the plaintiff, these fees may be added to the judgment amount against the defendant.

Issuing a Summons

The court must issue a summons commanding the defendant to appear for hearing or trial. Most courts require the plaintiff to prepare the summons form (DC 104) that is included in the form packet for DC 102a and to file it with the complaint. When the summons and complaint forms are filed, the court will "issue" the summons by dating and signing it. A summons must comply with MCR 2.102 and MCL 600.5735.

Getting the Summons and Complaint to the Tenant

After you have filed your complaint (form DC 102a), along with the summons (form DC 104) and the clerk has issued the summons, you must notify the defendant that you have filed a complaint against him or her. This is done by serving (delivering) the summons and complaint on the defendant. To make sure you serve the court papers as required, follow the instructions on the packet for the complaint form (DC 102a). See also MCR 4.201(D) and MCL 600.5735 for service requirements.

What if You Get a Summons and Complaint

If you are served with a summons (form DC 104) and complaint (form DC 102a), you must appear and answer the complaint by the date on the summons. You can appear and answer by either: 1) filing a written answer or motion and serving the plaintiff with that answer or motion; or 2) orally answering each allegation in the complaint at the hearing. See MCR 4.201(F) for details.

Pursuant to local court rule, the following courts require a written response to be filed with the court before the hearing/trial will be scheduled: 1st District Court (Monroe County), 2A District Court (Lenawee County), 12th District Court (Jackson County), 18th District Court (City of Westland), 81st District Court (Alcona, Arenac, Iosco, and Oscoda Counties), 82nd District Court (Ogemaw County), and 95B District Court (Dickinson and Iron Counties).

If you decide to file a written answer, a paper copy of the answer form is available from the court or you can complete it online (Answer to Complaint, Nonpayment of Rent, Landlord-Tenant, DC 111a). A responsive pleading (answer) must comply with the general rules for pleading in MCR 2.111. Also, if you want to present defenses to the statements made in the complaint, they must be included in the written answer. A defense means a reason you (the tenant/defendant) present to the court to oppose a plaintiff's (the landlord's) complaint and the relief that the plaintiff is requesting (usually a judgment of possession). You may want to consult an attorney to help you prepare your defenses. Some common defenses to a landlord's complaint for a nonpayment of rent eviction are:

- the landlord failed to follow the requirements for a demand for possession, which is usually grounds for dismissal of the complaint. See MCL 600.5716 and MCL 600.5718.

- the landlord's claim for unpaid rent is too high. You will need evidence to prove this, such as receipts, cancelled checks, money order tracer reports, or other proof of payment.

- a disagreement about the rental amount. You will need evidence to prove that the rental rate stated in the complaint is wrong, such as a lease, another agreement, or some other statement of the landlord that support your position.

- the landlord failed to properly repair and maintain the premises. See MCL 554.139, MCL 125.471, and MCL 600.5741.

You have the right to be represented by an attorney. You are entitled to a jury trial, but you must demand it and pay a jury fee of $50.00 when you make your first appearance and answer.

If you do not appear and answer as required, the court may enter a default judgment against you. This means the judge may grant a judgment for the plaintiff without hearing from you and, if requested in the complaint, an immediate order of eviction may be entered.

Preparing for the Hearing

To prepare for the hearing, gather the evidence you need to prove your case. This might include a receipt, guarantee, lease, contract, government inspection report, or accident report. If a damaged article is too big to bring with you, photographs can be presented as evidence. Any witnesses you would like to speak on your behalf should appear in court with you so you should contact them as soon as possible. Letters and affidavits are not permitted as evidence. More details are provided in the forms packets. See general information about hearings for directions on getting witnesses to appear.

Attending the Hearing

The hearing will usually take place at the location stated in the summons/notice to appear. It is important to be there on time. If you are the plaintiff (landlord) and are not in court when your case is called, the case may be dismissed. If you are the defendant (tenant) and are not in court when your case is called, a default judgment may be entered against you. This means that if the judge decides the plaintiff has a good claim, the plaintiff can obtain a judgment without a hearing because the defendant did not appear to challenge the complaint.

At the hearing, the landlord must prove: 1) that the tenant failed to pay rent, 2) that the tenant was given proper notice to either pay the rent or move out or vacate the premises, and 3) that the tenant did not pay the rent or move out or vacate the premises within 7 days of the notice.

Bring all your relevant papers or other evidence and make sure your witnesses arrive on time. Evidence that you present is subject to the Michigan Rules of Evidence. Witnesses will be allowed to tell the court about facts they know firsthand that support your evidence. See general information about hearings.

An eviction case can be heard by a judge or a jury, and the hearing will be recorded. The court clerk will call the case and both the plaintiff and the defendant will appear before the judge. The judge will ask the plaintiff to state the facts and law in support of the complaint. When the plaintiff has finished, the defendant will have an opportunity to respond. You should listen carefully. If you think someone is leaving something out or is misstating facts, you should be sure to tell the judge or jury.

When speaking to the judge, you should take time to tell what happened in your own words and state why you think the court should order what you want. You have the right to ask questions of each other and of all witnesses.

You may appeal the judge's decision to the circuit court. If you lose the case, you may be ordered to pay the court costs as allowed by MCL 600.5759 and you should be prepared to pay for this extra expense.

Judgment of the Court

The court prepares the Judgment, form DC 105, after the hearing/trial. The court may award a judgment for costs pursuant to MCL 600.5741 and MCL 600.5759. The court will also make sure that the judgment is given or sent to you. If the judgment is in favor of the landlord (plaintiff), it will give the tenant 10 days to pay the rent and costs or the landlord may obtain an order evicting the tenant. The judgment may also include a money award if one has been requested.

Evicting the Tenant

If the court entered a judgment that the plaintiff has the right to recover possession of the property and the defendant does not move out as stated in the judgment, the plaintiff can file an application with the court to have the defendant evicted as provided by MCL 600.5744. Follow the instructions on the Order of Eviction, form DC 107.

After an order of eviction is entered, the landlord must serve the order on the defendant as stated in Michigan Court Rule 2.602(D)(1). An order of eviction can only be enforced by those persons specified in Michigan Court Rule 3.106(B).

Collecting a Money Judgment

If a money judgment was ordered for damages and/or costs and is not paid when ordered, additional papers must be filed with the court to collect on the judgment by having wages or a bank account garnished or property seized. This cannot occur until 21 days after the judgment is entered. See information about collection.

Appendix 4 – Ohio Small Claims

This guide is for informational purposes only and should not be relied on for legal advice. If you need legal advice, contact an attorney.

This guide presents an overview of rules and procedures for small claims court. The specific rules and procedures in your court may vary from those presented here. Check with your court about local rules.

Introduction

This pamphlet describes small claims court in Ohio. It is designed to help those who plan to sue someone in small claims court or who are parties to a case in small claims court. While every effort has been made to present accurate information about small claims court in Ohio, you should also contact the court that may or will hear your case. It is possible that some laws have changed since this pamphlet was updated, and there are variations among different small claims courts. You need to know about local rules, procedures, and costs. Hopefully this pamphlet will give you a good idea about how small claims court works and what questions to ask your local court. Also keep in mind that everyone has the right to hire an attorney, including you and the other parties in your small claims case. While it is generally an advantage to be represented by an attorney, you will need to weigh that advantage against the cost. A brief consultation with an attorney may well be worth the cost.

What is small claims court?

Ohio law requires that each county and municipal court establish a small claims division, generally known as small claims court. (See chapter 1925 of the Ohio Revised Code.) The purpose of the small claims court is to resolve minor disputes fairly, quickly, and inexpensively. The procedures in small claims court are simpler than in other court cases. Hearings are informal; there is no jury; cases are decided either by the municipal court or county court judge, or by a "magistrate" (a qualified attorney appointed by the judge); court costs are lower than in other cases. Many small claims courts hold evening sessions and small claims courts in large metropolitan areas may have neighborhood offices.

The relative simplicity of small claims court makes it easier for people to handle their cases without attorneys. However, anyone who wishes to may bring an attorney to small claims court.

What cases can a small claims court handle?

Small claims cases are like other lawsuits, except that the amounts involved are generally too small to make the expense of regular court proceedings worthwhile. A small claims court can resolve many common disputes that involve modest amounts of money. Typical small claims court cases include claims by tenants to recover security deposits, claims by landlords for unpaid rent or damage to their property, claims by buyers for damages from defective merchandise, claims by business people and trades people for unpaid bills, claims by car owners for damage sustained in minor accidents, claims by employees, babysitters, maids, and handypersons for unpaid wages. There are limits on claims that can be resolved in small claims court:

The claims must be for money only. Small claims court cannot issue restraining orders, protection orders or injunctions, cannot grant divorces, and cannot order someone to return property. Small claims court can only resolve claims that ask for money.

A claim cannot exceed $3,000 (not including any interest and court costs claimed). The claim itself can be for at most $3,000, and counter- or cross-claims that may be filed can only be for $3,000 (each) or less.

Regardless of the amount of money involved, a small claims court cannot handle certain types of lawsuits: lawsuits based on libel, slander, and malicious prosecution, lawsuits seeking punitive or exemplary damages, or lawsuits brought by an assignee or agent (such as a lawsuit brought by an insurance company on behalf of a policy holder; however, government entities can bring certain lawsuits through an agent).

Small claims court cannot resolve claims against the agencies of the State of Ohio or against the United States government and its agencies.

If you have questions about whether your case fits these criteria, you may need legal advice from an attorney. Court staff may be able to answer questions about 1 and 2, but any doubts about issue 3 need to be resolved with legal advice.

Cases that initially fit the small claims criteria may be transferred out of small claims court:

If a case starts with a claim for $3,000 or less but then comes to include claims that exceed $3,000, the case will be transferred to the civil division of municipal or county court. If one of the parties to a case requests it, a case may be transferred to the civil division of the municipal or county court.

Who can sue or be sued in small claims court?

In general, anyone 18 years or older can sue or be sued in small claims court. A minor under the age of 18 may file a lawsuit through a parent or guardian.

Corporations, certain partnerships, and limited liability companies may sue and be sued in small claims court. If you are an officer or an employee of such an organization and are involved in a small claims court case on your organization's behalf, you should seek the advice of an attorney before you file any document with the court. You may present evidence concerning your side in a dispute, but you may not engage in advocacy. If you advocate in court on behalf of your organization, you may violate rules about the unauthorized practice of law—even if all you do is fill out forms and file papers. To avoid such a violation, contact an attorney to find out what you may and may not do on your organization's behalf. Please note that court staff may not advise you on this issue.

When you file against a business, you must determine whether it is a sole proprietorship, a partnership, or a corporation. To find out, contact the Ohio Secretary of State's office—call 614-466-2655 or visit www.sos.state.oh.us. You might also find out from the county auditor, who maintains records of vendor's licenses, or from the county recorder, who may have records about partnerships.

Where do I file my claim?

Your claim must be filed in the small claims division of a municipal court or county court that has jurisdiction in your case. To determine which court has jurisdiction, you use one of two criteria:

A small claims court has jurisdiction if the transaction or incident on which your claim is based took place in that court's territory.

Regardless of where the transaction or incident took place, a small claims court also has jurisdiction if the defendant (the person or organization being sued)—or any one defendant, if there is more than one—lives or has his or her or its principal place of business in the court's territory. This means that more than one court may have jurisdiction in your case. If so, you can choose which of those courts to file in. Check the territorial boundaries of each court that may have jurisdiction. You can do this by calling each court that may have jurisdiction and asking whether the locations of 1 and 2 above are within the court's jurisdiction. File your claim with a court that has jurisdiction.

How do I file my claim?

You begin a lawsuit on a small claim by filing a formal statement of claim with the small claims court. Your statement must contain a description of the nature and amount of your claim.

Before you file the formal claim, it is a good idea (but not required) to make a last effort to settle the dispute. You can do this by sending the potential defendant(s) a letter by certified mail, return receipt requested. Your letter can be elaborate or simple. At a minimum, your letter should summarize the basic facts of your claim and state the amount of money you want. After reading your letter, the defendant might pay the claim or offer a sensible compromise. If you decide to go ahead with a small claims lawsuit, contact the municipal court or county court that has jurisdiction. Ask about the court's business hours, the cost of filing a small claims case, and whether there are any other local requirements for filing a small claims case. Remember that court staff may not give you legal advice or in any way assess the claim you intend to file. But they may and can explain what you need to bring with you to file a claim.

If your claim cannot be filed in that court, ask for the name, address, and telephone number of the proper court and contact that court. When you go to the court to file your case, you need to bring at least the following information:

The full name (and business name, if applicable), address, and telephone number of the defendant;

A list of the evidence you have that supports your claim. Some courts ask that you file your evidence with your claim but others do not—ask before you arrive at court to file, and keep copies of anything you file;

The names and addresses of all of your witnesses; and enough cash to pay the filing fee.

Your court may ask for additional information or items—be sure to ask before you arrive to file your claim. In most courts you make your claim by completing a form designated for small claims. Be sure to fill in the form completely. Use clear language. Write or print legibly. State the nature, circumstances, and amount of your claim as briefly as possible.

Pay special attention to several points.

When you state the amount of your claim, consider whether you want interest on any judgment and reimbursement for all court costs. If you do, be sure your complaint asks for damages, interest on your damages, and reimbursement of all court costs, including those incurred in enforcing a judgment (i.e., in getting payment from the other party). Note that Ohio law does not permit you to recover wages for time lost for preparing or filing your case or for appearing in court.

Find out whether the defendant is on active military duty: federal law provides some protection for those who are on active duty, and the court will ask about the defendant's military status.

The court must officially notify the defendant that he or she is being sued, and it is your responsibility to provide an address where the defendant can be reached. The official notice must be delivered to—or "served on"—the defendant(s). The usual way to accomplish service is certified mail to the defendant's home or business address. The return receipt, signed by anyone 16 years of age or older, will provide proof of service. The case can then proceed. However, if the certified letter is returned undelivered, the case cannot proceed. If that happens, check with court staff about other ways to accomplish service.

How much does it cost?

Each court has established a filing fee. Call the court and ask what the fee is. If you plan to subpoena a witness, ask for information about the costs required. If you cannot afford these fees, you may file an affidavit of indigency with the court and ask that your fees be waived. Court staff can provide you with instructions for how to file such an affidavit. The court will let you know whether your affidavit was accepted. If the court is satisfied that you cannot afford these fees, you may file without fees. But if the court is not satisfied, you will need to pay the fees. Generally, you may be able to recover all of your out-of-pocket court fees, together with interest. Be sure to ask for reimbursement of your court costs along with your demand for recovery of your damages and interest.

How long does it take?

When you file a case, the court is required to set an initial hearing date that is no sooner than 15 days after the filing date and no later than 40 days after the filing date. Subsequent developments may delay that date somewhat, but in general you can estimate that your case will be heard within 40 days.

I've been sued! What do I do?

If someone has filed a small claim against you, the court will send you official notice. The notice and its attachments will give you important information: the name and address of the plaintiff, the basis and amount of the claim, the name and address of the court in which the claim was filed, and the date and time you must appear in court to resolve the claim.

The official notice from the court will also tell you how to respond to the plaintiff's claim. Of course, the nature of your response depends on what you think about the claim that is being made. But whatever you think, be sure to carefully follow the instructions from the court about how to file the response you believe is appropriate.

Some courts require that you respond to the claim against you in writing; others do not. If the official notice leaves you in doubt, contact the court to find out. Even if the court does not require a written response, it is always wise to prepare a written summary.

Whether or not you file a written statement, and whether or not you concede the claim against you, you must appear at the hearing on the date and time stated in the official notice. Of course, if the claim is fully settled and formally dismissed, the hearing will be cancelled. See "What if the claim is settled before the hearing?" on page 8.

Below are general options for responding to a claim filed against you. The instructions provided with the court's official notice that you have been sued might require that you respond in a different way. If there is a conflict between the suggestion below and the official notice, follow the instructions that accompany the official notice.

Depending on what you believe about the claim made against you, you have several options.

If you believe the plaintiff's claim is fair, you may pay the plaintiff the full amount of the claim, plus court costs, and that will be the end of the matter. See "What if the claim is settled before the hearing?" See Below.

If you believe part of the plaintiff's claim is fair, you may admit that part of the claim and deny the rest.

If you believe the plaintiff's claim is completely unfair, you may deny that you owe anything.

If you believe the plaintiff actually owes you money, you may answer with a claim of your own called a "counterclaim."

If the plaintiff has named multiple defendants and you have a claim against one of those defendants, you may file a claim against that defendant, a "cross-claim."

If the plaintiff's claim does not include some parties that are necessary to resolve the lawsuit, you may ask the court to bring in such other persons or entities by making a "third-party claim."

If you want to file counterclaims, cross-claims and third-party claims, ask the court about how to file them. There are several issues to consider:

Your claims: you must explain why you believe each claim is justified and be prepared to present evidence. Remember that court staff may not assess whether your claims are good, but they can provide forms and explain the procedure for filing your claim(s).

Amounts: if you believe the plaintiff or some other defendant(s) owe you money, you should consider asking for your damages, interest on your damages, and all court costs, including those incurred in enforcing a judgment on the counter- or cross-claim.

Third parties: if you believe any additional party or parties should be brought into the claim because they are liable for all or part of the claim—either along with you or instead of you—you need to file a third party claim. Be sure to state the complete name and address of each additional party who should be brought into the claim, and your reasons why that party, or parties, should be brought into the claim.

Deadlines: Counter- and cross-claims must be filed with the court in which the original claim was filed and at least seven (7) days prior to the date of the hearing on plaintiff's original claim. Ask the court about deadlines for third party claims.

Official notice: all parties must be officially notified about all claims in which they are involved—all claims must be "served on" them. Be sure to ask court staff how any counter- or cross- or third party claims you file are served on or sent to all other parties. The court may send the counterclaim and/or cross-claim to all parties, or may require you to send them and present proof that the parties did receive them. (For example, you may be required to serve parties by certified mail and present return receipts as proof.)

However you wish to respond, make sure you do so as soon as possible. Unless the instructions that accompany the official notice specify another requirement, and unless your response includes any of the additional claims above, the last day it should get to the court is the last work day before the date that the official notice says you must appear at a hearing to defend the claim. This means that if, for example, a hearing is scheduled for Monday, August 6, you should get your response to the court by Friday, August 3. Be sure to call the court if you have problems submitting the response on time.

Finally, remember an important formality: all your communications about the case must clearly show the case number that appears on the notice you received from the court. If your response does not include this number, the clerk may not be able to file your response in the proper case file and the suit may be delayed or the judge may not know your position.

Some procedures vary from court to court. Be sure to read and follow the instructions that accompany the official notice from the court. And if you have doubts about procedures and deadlines, contact the court and ask.

What is mediation?

In nearly all of the larger courts, and in many of the smaller courts as well, the court will make available a mediator to assist you and the other party to try to work out a settlement. The mediator is not a judge and will not decide your case or give you legal advice.

A mediation hearing is a court-supervised conference where the plaintiff and defendant are given an opportunity to discuss all aspects of their dispute and to settle it without having a formal court hearing about the legal claim. Mediation hearings are confidential. If the mediation fails and the case proceeds to a formal court hearing, the information revealed in the mediation may not be used in court.

Take full advantage of the opportunity to participate in a mediation hearing! Mediation hearings are less formal than court hearings and can consider a broader range of issues surrounding the legal claim: it may be the only chance you have to air all of your concerns, to hear the concerns of the other party, and to come to an agreement that concerns issues other than the money one party may owe another. Through mediation, you may arrive at a solution that better suits your needs than a court-imposed judgment.

Mediation is generally available at several stages of the case: you may be able to have a court mediation hearing before you file the case, and you may be able to schedule a mediation up to and including the day of the court hearing. Some courts require you to appear at a mediation hearing. Check the local rules of your court, and ask if you are uncertain.

What if the claim is settled before the hearing?

If you have filed a small claim, and the defendant pays you an agreed upon amount to settle your claim, you should notify the court in writing. Be sure to ask the court whether you need to fill out a specific form or can write your own statement noting that your claim has been settled. Your written notice of settlement will be made part of the record and your case will then be dismissed.

Note that the court will not return any fees or other court costs that you have paid. Any settlement you agree to with the defendant should be made with consideration given to these fees.

If you have been sued, and you have made an agreement with the plaintiff that you believe settles the entire claim, ask for written confirmation from the plaintiff and for a copy of the notice of settlement as filed with the court. If you have not received a notice from the court that your case has been dismissed before the scheduled hearing date of your case, contact the court to make sure that your case has indeed been completely settled and dismissed.

How do I prepare my case?

Whether you are the plaintiff or the defendant, your job at the formal hearing (trial) is to give the judge the facts and convince the judge that he or she should decide in your favor.

Before the hearing, collect your evidence, contact your witnesses, and make a written outline of your case.

Your evidence may include:

- your testimony,
- the testimony of witnesses,
- written items such as sales receipts, contracts, leases, warranties, promissory notes, IOUs, memos, notes, letters, postal return receipts, unclaimed letter notices, etc.,

- items relevant to the case—for example, a piece of faulty merchandise on which your claim or defense is based,
- photos or diagrams, perhaps of the damage to some item or of the scene of the incident.

In summary, anything that can support your case may be useful as evidence.

However: check with your court about any local rules concerning evidence. Many courts do not allow affidavits—written statements from someone concerning some facts of the case—but require all witnesses to appear in person. Many courts require you to bring several copies of any written items, photos, etc. It is your responsibility to make sure that the evidence you intend to present will be acceptable in court.

Certain kinds of witness testimony may be especially useful as evidence. For example, when poor or incomplete workmanship is an important question a professional repairperson could be a good witness. Useful witnesses may also include friends, neighbors, or bystanders who are familiar with some aspect of the incident or transaction.

It is necessary and appropriate to talk to your witnesses before the hearing. You have to ask them what they know, and if they will come and testify. When you talk to witnesses, tell them to testify truthfully.

Remember that your witnesses may also need to answer questions from the other party. Shortly before the hearing, contact your witnesses again to make sure they agree to testify and confirm the time and place of the hearing.

If a witness will not voluntarily testify, you can ask the court to order the witness to testify. Such an order is called a subpoena.

Ask the court how to request a subpoena—you need to know about deadlines (ask well in advance of the hearing date!), about service (how to make sure the witness will receive the official notice of the subpoena), and about any additional costs to you for the subpoena.

How much evidence is enough? There is no easy answer—in some cases, your testimony alone may be enough, but it is likely you will need other testimony or other evidence. One way to consider how much

evidence is needed is to assume that you are the judge and that you do not know the facts of the case, and then ask yourself, "What evidence would a party in this case need to present to convince me that the facts require a decision in his, her, or its favor?"

More important than the quantity of evidence is the quality of your evidence. Your witnesses should be believable—they should be persons who have direct knowledge of the facts they testify to and who are trustworthy individuals. Items like receipts, contracts, pictures and other things should be clear and understandable, and there should be no room for doubt that they are what you claim they are. Remember that the other party may present witnesses and evidence that conflict with yours. You want to ensure that your case is supported by the best testimony and evidence.

When you have gathered your evidence, including your own testimony and the testimony of other witnesses, write an outline of the points you wish to make to support your claim or defense. List your evidence and witnesses in the order you wish to present them. A good way to present your version of the incident or transaction is in the sequence it actually happened, just like you would tell a story. In this way, the separate bits of testimony and other evidence will fit together as a complete, understandable account of the incident or transaction.

What if I do not appear at the hearing?

If you fail to appear you may immediately lose, regardless of how well supported your claim or defense might be.

If a party does not appear at a hearing, and that party has not given the judge a good reason, the judge can and quite possibly will decide the case in favor of the party attending the scheduled hearing.

If you cannot attend the hearing on the date the court has scheduled, contact the court as soon as you know you cannot attend. Most courts require that you submit a request to postpone the hearing in writing—either in person or via fax. Another hearing date may be scheduled. If you are prevented from attending at the last minute, or if you will be late, call the court and explain the situation.

What do I do at the hearing?

The hearing is your day in court—your opportunity to present your claim, defense, counterclaim, cross-claim, or third-party claim. Whether you win or lose, you are assured of a fair hearing. Both you and the other party will have an opportunity to present your case and your evidence to the court.

Bring your evidence and witnesses with you. Bring enough copies of your documents, pictures, etc. Make sure your witnesses appear in person—most courts do not accept written statements from witnesses and will not allow witnesses to appear by phone. (One exception may be cost estimates; if it is relevant in your case, ask the court whether written statements of costs are acceptable as evidence.)

Your case is likely to be one of many small claims cases scheduled for an extended session. Wait your turn, and respond when your case is called.

The plaintiff goes first. The judge will ask the plaintiff to give his, her, or its version of the case. After the plaintiff is finished, the judge will ask the defendant for his, her, or its version of the case.

Be brief and stick to the facts. Use the outline you wrote when you prepared your case. Emphasize the points in your favor, and explain the points against you. The judge may interrupt you with questions. Answer the questions directly, politely, and to the best of your knowledge.

Be polite—not just to the judge, but also to all witnesses and to the other party. Whatever happens, control your temper. Good manners, a calm attitude, and an orderly presentation promote a fair and efficient hearing and make a positive impression.

You will probably be nervous. Relax, be yourself, and present your case in the way that comes most easily to you. The judge knows you are not a lawyer and will make allowances. Listen carefully to what the judge says or asks and respond accordingly.

After hearing both sides, the judge (or magistrate) will make his or her decision. The judge may state his or her decision at the end of the hearing, or may state that the claim is "heard and submitted" and issue a written decision at a later date. Be sure to ask the court how you will be notified of the decision.

What if I disagree with the judgment?

If you disagree with the judgment in your case, it may be possible for you to continue the process. The practices and deadlines in this area vary from court to court, so you need to ask the court how to proceed.

You can ask the judge or magistrate to reconsider your case. Ask the court how to file for reconsideration.

If a magistrate heard your case, you may file written objections within fourteen (14) days of the filing of the magistrate's decision. Your objections will be reviewed by a judge of the court according to the procedures established in that court. The judge may affirm and adopt the magistrate's report, or modify and enter a judgment, or order a new trial. Ask the court how to file objections to a magistrate's decision.

If a judge decided your case, you may appeal to the court of appeals that has jurisdiction over the municipal or county court that heard your case. It is very unusual for small claims to be appealed, but appeals are possible. Ask your court how to file an appeal.

If you are considering filing objections or an appeal, you need to be aware of three things.

Fees. You may have to pay additional filing fees—in some cases for objections to a magistrate's decision, and in all cases for an appeal to a higher court.

Record. Generally, your small claims court hearing will have been recorded—perhaps on audio tape or perhaps some other way. If you file objections or an appeal, you may have to pay the costs for a court reporter to produce a written transcript from the recording.

Costs and complexity. The appeals process is complex and can be costly. Before you begin it, you should consult with an attorney about the merits of your legal claim.

What about payment?

If the judgment in your case means that the other party owes you money, continue on to the next section to learn about how to collect the money.

If the judgment in your case means that you owe money to the other party, contact the person or entity that won and attempt to negotiate the amount and terms of payment. When you pay, ask for a written receipt that states clearly that you and the other party are settling the judgment in full.

If you cannot afford to pay the entire judgment immediately, you can ask the judge for permission to pay in installments. If your money problems are really serious, there are some alternatives available that are summarized in "What if I need help paying the judgment?" on page 14.

How do I get my money?

You yourself must take action to force payment of your judgment.

The court will not get your money for you. However, if you take the required steps, including paying the relevant court costs, the court will help you enforce your judgment (get your money). This section will describe your collection options, and the next several sections will explain how to get the court's help.

The best way to collect on a judgment is voluntary payment by the judgment debtor (the person who must pay under the judgment). If the judgment debtor does not voluntarily pay, you can get help from the court in one of three ways: you can garnish the judgment debtor's personal earnings or bank account, obtain a "judgment lien" against the judgment debtor's real estate, or attach and sell of some of the judgment debtor's personal property.

Voluntary payment. If possible, make arrangements with the judgment debtor to pay the judgment, either all at once or in installments. The court may order that payment be made by a certain date or in installments.

Garnishment. If the judgment debtor will not pay voluntarily, the usual method of forcing payment is garnishment. In garnishment, the court orders the judgment debtor's employer or bank to satisfy the judgment by paying from the judgment debtor's earnings or bank account to the court, which in turn pays the money to the judgment creditor (the person who is owed money under the judgment).

There are limitations on how much the employer or bank can pay the court. First, the amount cannot exceed the judgment. Second, a bank can pay only the money in the account. Third, if the source of the funds in the bank account can be directly traced to wages, social security payments or certain pension payments, these funds cannot be garnished. Fourth, in general, an employer cannot pay more than 25% of the judgment debtor's net earnings.

It is possible that the judgment debtor whose wages you seek to garnish has other judgments pending. If so, garnishments will become effective in the order the debtor's employer receives them. A garnishment, once in effect, will remain in effect for at least six (6) months, or until the debt is paid, whichever occurs first. Thus, you may have to "wait your turn," so to speak, for your garnishment to take effect.

Judgment Lien. Also, you may obtain a judgment lien on any real estate the judgment debtor may own or acquire. A judgment lien does not automatically force the payment of money, but it gives you a security interest—like a mortgage—in the judgment debtor's real property. See "How can I obtain a judgment lien? What does it do?" on page 13.

Attachment. Another method of forcing payment is attachment. Under attachment, the court orders some of the judgment debtor's personal property (for example, a car worth more than a certain amount, a boat, a large screen television, a valuable collection or something else) seized and sold to pay the judgment. Attachment is more complicated and time-consuming than garnishment, and often more costly as well. If you are considering this option, you may need to consult an attorney. To initiate garnishment, attachment or judgment lien, you will need the court's help.

How can I get help to enforce my judgment?

You can get help to enforce your judgment by contacting the court that issued the judgment in your favor or by contacting an attorney. If you have obtained a judgment in a small claims court, the court will help you enforce your judgment—but only *after* you have paid the court costs. However, while you have to pay these costs up front, if you asked for court costs when you stated your claim (or counterclaim, cross-claim, or third-party claim), you may be reimbursed for such costs if the proceedings to enforce your judgment are successful.

After you have paid the court costs, the court will explain the necessary procedures, give you the proper forms, and help you institute a garnishment, attachment, or other proceeding to collect your judgment.

If it is necessary to take court action to collect your judgment, you will need both patience and persistence. The law allows judgment debtors to keep certain items or assets (or portions of assets) so that judgment debtors have the basics with which to support themselves. Creditors cannot take these exempt items or assets.

How can I find property to garnish or attach?

The easiest way to find the judgment debtor's property is to have the court order the judgment debtor to answer a standard questionnaire about his, her, or its property and finances.

Wait thirty (30) days after you obtain your judgment. If, in that time, the judgment has not been paid, and no arrangements have been made to pay it, go to the court which issued the judgment and ask for a "debtor's examination" of the judgment debtor. Under a debtor's examination, the court orders the judgment debtor to identify his, her, or its assets, liabilities, and earnings.

Some courts ask you to start the process by sending a 15-day demand letter to the judgment debtor. Courts will have instructions for how to do this, and may have forms.

Some courts conduct debtor's examination hearings, which you may attend, while others send a form to the judgment debtor. If the judgment debtor fails to appear or to submit the information in writing, he, she or it may be found in contempt of court and fined or jailed, or both. The debtor's examination will provide the information you need to take action to enforce your judgment. The information will reveal, for example, where defendant works and lives, where his, her, or its bank accounts are, whether he, she, or it owns real estate, etc.

How can I obtain a judgment lien? What does it do?

You can get a judgment lien by filing a "certificate of judgment" with the clerk of the common pleas court in any county where the judgment debtor owns real estate.

Obtain a certificate of judgment from the court that heard your case. You will pay a modest fee for preparation of the certificate.

Using the information from the debtor's examination (see previous section), determine where the judgment debtor owns real estate. The county auditor may also have information that will help you with this.

Contact the clerk of the common pleas court in the county where the judgment debtor owns real estate, and inquire about how to file the certificate with that court. You will have to pay another modest fee to file the certificate.

If the judgment debtor owns real estate in more than one county, you can file certificates of judgment in all those counties. If you wish to file certificates of judgment in multiple counties, be sure to obtain sufficient certificates of judgment from the clerk of the court that heard your case. Usually, a certificate is filed in the county where the judgment debtor lives and, therefore, presumably owns a home.

When filed, the certificate of judgment imposes a lien on the judgment debtor's real estate that is located in the county where the certificate is filed.

A judgment lien based on a certificate of judgment automatically expires after 5 years. If the judgment debtor still has not paid at that time, you can renew the judgment lien by getting a new certificate of judgment.

A judgment lien by itself does not get your money. You have to foreclose the lien to get your money—just like foreclosing a mortgage. Foreclosing a lien is a complicated procedure; in general, it will require the services of an attorney.

Nevertheless, a judgment lien is still useful. If the judgment debtor wants to sell or refinance the real estate that is subject to your lien, he, she, or it will have to pay your judgment in order to give clear title to a buyer.

If your judgment is paid in full, including court costs and interest, if any, it is your duty to see that the judgment lien is cancelled. If your judgment is paid in connection with the private sale of the real estate subject to your lien, the buyer's lender, if any, may file the required notice of cancellation for you.

What if I need help paying the judgment?

If you are in serious financial trouble, because of lawsuits or other reasons, you have several options: trusteeship, debt scheduling agreement, wage earner plan, or bankruptcy. However, if this is your situation, you should get professional help. Court staff may know where you can turn for free help with resolving financial trouble. The following summary is merely a starting point.

If you fail to pay the judgment against you, you may receive a "15-day demand," also called "Notice Of Court Proceeding To Collect Debt." This is sent to you by the person who won the judgment against you, and it is his or her first step in asking the court for help to collect the money. The notice will include brief explanations of trusteeships and debt scheduling agreements.

Trusteeship is an arrangement made through the municipal or county court where you live (or where you work, if you do not live in Ohio). A trusteeship arranges for part of your earnings to be regularly divided and applied to your liquidated debts (debts where the final amount is known) until these debts are paid.

To be eligible for a trusteeship, you must have received a 15-day demand or notice of collection, which is the first step in garnishment.

You may need to pay a fee for the trusteeship, usually a percentage of the amount to be administered.

If you enter a trusteeship, garnishment will be stopped and your creditors will generally be held off as long as you faithfully follow the trusteeship plan. However, certain of your creditors can object to the establishment of a trusteeship.

A trusteeship does not prevent creditors from taking certain actions. For example, creditors can continue to obtain judgments, and can, pursuant to court order, attach and sell property that is not exempt.

A debt scheduling agreement developed through an approved consumer credit counseling service is similar to a trusteeship. In summary, a person who wishes to establish a debt scheduling agreement meets with a representative of an approved consumer credit counseling service to determine if an agreement can be arranged. If an agreement can be arranged, the person—the debtor—deposits the non-essential portion of his or her income with the service, and the service distributes the funds to creditors pursuant to the agreement. Approved consumer credit counseling services do not charge debtors for the services they provide.

You are eligible for a debt scheduling agreement regardless of whether or not you have received a 15-day demand.

Creditors voluntarily participate in the debt scheduling plan. Once an agreement is established, creditors may not garnish the wages of the debtor as long as the debtor faithfully follows the agreement.

Creditors who have accepted the plan may take other legal actions to collect the debt. For example, they may garnish bank accounts, and certain creditors may attach and sell the property that the judgment debtor pledged as security and failed to pay for. But in general, creditors who participate in debt scheduling agreements will not use these and other legal collection devices as long as debtors follow the debt scheduling agreements.

Two further options require you to work with the federal courts:

Wage earner plans are administered by the federal courts. A wage earner plan is similar to a trusteeship in that part of the debtor's earnings is regularly applied to his or her financial obligations until those debts are paid. Under federal law, creditors are held off as long as the debtor follows the plan.

Bankruptcies are also administered by the federal courts. In bankruptcy, the debtor's property is divided among the creditors, and most of the debtor's obligations are completely discharged, even if his or her property is not worth enough to pay all the debts.

Where can I get more information?

While this section offers some sources of additional information, it does not list all possible sources of information. For example, you can contact a lawyer, the lawyer referral service of a local bar association, or the local legal aid society.

If you need more information or assistance on filing or defending a small claim, collecting a judgment on a small claim, filing for trusteeship, or entering a debt scheduling agreement, contact the small claims court where the claim will be filed, or has been filed.

If you are thinking of filing for a wage earner plan or for bankruptcy, contact a lawyer, the lawyer referral service of a local bar association, or the local legal aid society.

Appendix 5 – Michigan Small Claims

This guide is for informational purposes only and should not be relied on for legal advice. If you need legal advice, contact an attorney.

This guide presents an overview of rules and procedures for small claims court. The specific rules and procedures in your court may vary from those presented here. Check with your court about local rules.

Introduction

The following provides general information about small claims. You may want to consult an attorney for legal advice, but an attorney cannot represent you in a small claims matter. This means you must file court documents, appear in court, and pursue collection of any judgment without an attorney. For specific information about how to file a small claims case and what else you need to do, see the Small Claims Self-Help Center on the MI.gov website.

Is the Small Claims Division Right for You?

Before you file a claim in the small claims division of the district court, you should decide whether it is the right "court" for you. There are a number of things to consider, from the amount of your claim to your ability to "represent" yourself in court.

The small claims division of the district court is a "court of limited jurisdiction." There is no small claims division of the municipal court. The small claims division of the district court cannot award more than $5,000, except for court costs and interest, even if your claim is worth more. If you do not want to waive your right to any amount over $5,000, you will have to bring your claim in the general civil division of the district court (for claims up to $25,000) or the circuit court (for claims over $25,000). In the small claims division your case may be heard by a district court judge or a district court attorney magistrate.

The small claims division can only handle certain kinds of claims, such as simple cases to recover money, perform a contract, set aside a contract, or change a contract. For example, the small claims division can hear a dispute between a landlord and a tenant about the return of a security deposit, or it can hear a case involving a car accident where insurance did not cover the damages to a car. The small claims division cannot hear cases of fraud, libel, slander, assault, battery, or other intentional wrongs. See MCL 600.8424(1). Although the small claims division cannot hear these intentional wrongs, it may still hear some intentional wrongdoing cases such as actions for insufficient funds (bounced checks) MCL 600.2952(6), Consumer Protection Act actions MCL 445.901 *et seq.*, and recreational trespass MCL 324.73109.

In a small claims case, the parties cannot have attorneys represent them. You cannot have a jury trial. In addition, the district court judge's decision is final and cannot be appealed. However, if the case is heard by a district court attorney magistrate, the decision may be appealed to the district court judge for a new hearing in the small claims division. If either party objects to these conditions, the case will be transferred to the general civil division of the district court for a hearing.

If you take your case to the small claims division, you have to be able to tell the district court judge or district court attorney magistrate why you are entitled to the relief you are requesting. You have to be able to answer questions in court and you have to gather evidence to present your claim. You need to be able to speak in public with people watching you. Even if you are feeling uncomfortable or stressed by the situation, you must be calm and able to think and speak in court in front of the judge or magistrate and your opponent. If you cannot do this, you should consider filing your case in a different court and having an attorney represent you.

Either side can request that a small claims case be removed to the regular district court civil division. If that occurs, all parties may have attorneys. Processing of the case then follows the pattern of a regular civil case and the decision may be appealed to the circuit court.

Should You Try to Settle Instead of Going to Court?

Before you file a case in the small claims division of the district court, you should think about the person or organization you are suing and the likelihood of getting money from that person if you get a money judgment. Does the person or organization have money or is the person or organization likely to have money in the future? For example, a retired person on social security without savings has a limited income and will not have more money in the future. Social security benefits are exempt from garnishment, so you are unlikely to collect money in this situation even if you get a money judgment in your favor. Also, it is important to realize that if the district court judge orders a money judgment, the person or organization might not automatically pay the money and court costs. You may have to take additional steps to obtain your money. One of the ways to collect your money is to garnish wages, a bank account, or a state income tax refund.

You should consider the possibility of losing your case and that you may be ordered to pay a judgment instead. This may be hard to think about unemotionally because people often confuse what is fair or moral with what is legal. Before you go to court, you should look realistically at what happened and talk with other people about your case to see how they react. If it is possible you might lose your case, you have to think about how you will pay a judgment.

Going to Court

If you decide to go to court, the procedures for small claims are simple, but they have to be followed. For additional information about how to file a small claims case and what else you need to do, see the Small Claims Self-Help Center.

Small Claims - Self Help

The following information will take you through the steps necessary in a proceeding in the small claims division of the district court. Online help is also available from Michigan Legal Help to prepare forms through an automated interview process and to provide toolkits with legal articles, FAQs, procedure, and other resources

Statutes and Court Rules

Statutes and court rules associated with small claims proceedings are: MCL 600.8401 through MCL 600.8427, MCL 600.8302, and MCR 4.301 through MCR 4.306.

Using Court Forms

Court forms are available for use in small claims proceedings. These forms follow the procedures stated in the Michigan Compiled Laws and Michigan Court Rules and can be used without the assistance of an attorney. Instructions for completing and using some of the forms are included.

When completing a form online, you must print the number of copies you will need for filing with the court and serving on the parties. See the upper right-hand corner of each form for this information. If you do not provide the court with the correct number of copies, the court might reject the form for nonconformance under the authority of Michigan Court Rule 8.119(C). Unless specifically required by court rule or statute, the court is not responsible for making copies of forms for you.

How to Begin a Small Claims Case

If you cannot resolve your dispute through settlement negotiations or mediation, you can file a claim against the person or business in the small claims division of district court. To start the case, an "affidavit and claim form" must be filed with the clerk of the district court. Details about how to complete the form and who can complete it are included with the Affidavit and Claim, Small Claims (form DC 84). You can go to the court and tell the clerk you want to file a small claims case, and the clerk will give you an Affidavit and Claim form to complete. Or you can complete the form online through this website, http://courts.mi.gov, print it, and bring it to the court.

Small claims cases should be filed either where the cause of action arose (for example, where the transaction or dispute took place), where the person or business you are suing is located (for example, where the defendant resides or is employed). If you are suing more than one person or business, the suit cannot be filed where the claim arose but must be filed in the district court where any of the persons live or where any of the businesses operate.

There is a fee for filing a small claims case. The cost of filing the lawsuit with the small claims division of the district court is $25 for claims up to $600, $45 for claims over $600 up to $1,750, and $65 for claims over $1,750 up to $5,000. The plaintiff is responsible for paying the filing fee and other required fees or costs (postage costs or fees for serving the claim on the defendant). The amount of the fees can be included as part of the judgment against the defendant (the person you are suing) if the judge decides in your favor.

The defendant may offer to settle out of court after learning you have filed a suit. If you settle the matter out of court, you can either voluntarily dismiss your lawsuit or obtain a judgment. If you want an enforceable judgment, the terms of your agreement must be spelled out in writing and signed by both you and the defendant. A copy of the agreement must be filed with the court.

Sending Notice of the Claim to the Defendant

The court must make sure that the defendant receives a copy of the affidavit and claim form (DC 84) along with notice to appear and answer before a district court judge or district court attorney magistrate. The court must also notify the plaintiff to appear at the time and place specified in the notice. This notice must comply with MCR 4.303 and MCL 600.8404.

Getting the Affidavit and Claim to the Defendant

After the affidavit and claim form (DC 84) is filed and the clerk has prepared the notice, the court will serve the affidavit and claim and notice on the defendant by either certified mail or personal service. The plaintiff must pay for this service. See MCL 600.8405 and MCR 4.303 for information on service requirements.

What if you Get a Small Claims Affidavit and Claim?

If you are served with an affidavit and claim from the small claims division of the district court, you are called the defendant. You have several ways to respond:

If you want to deny the claim, you must appear in court on the trial date, bringing with you any evidence you have to support your denial. Although not required, you can also file a written answer with the court. You can use DC 03 for this purpose.

If you want an attorney to represent you, you should tell the court before the trial, and the case will be transferred from the small claims division to the regular district court. See MCL 600.8408 and form DC 86.

If you want a jury trial, you must demand one before the trial, and the case will be removed from the small claims division to the regular district court. See MCL 600.8408 and form DC 86.

If you have a claim against the person who is suing you, you can also file a counterclaim. Your written counterclaim should be filed with the court and served by first-class mail to the person suing you.

If you want a judgment in excess of $5,000, you must demand that the case be removed from the small claims division to the regular district court. See MCL 600.8408 and form DC 86.

If you want to reserve the right to appeal any adverse decision to the circuit court, you must demand that the case be removed from the small claims division to the regular district court. See MCL 600.8408 and form DC 86.

If you fail to appear for the trial, the court will probably enter a default judgment against you. This means the judge may grant a judgment for the plaintiff without hearing your response to the claim.

The entry of a judgment against you may appear on your credit report.

Preparing for the Trial

On the trial date, any of the following may happen:

If both the plaintiff and the defendant appear, the judge may recommend that the parties go to mediation and the case may be adjourned. If either party does not want to attempt mediation, the trial will proceed.

Either party may request that the case be removed from the small claims division. In that situation, the trial will not be held and the small claims case will be treated like a regular civil case and decided later.

If the plaintiff does not appear and the defendant does appear, the case may be dismissed.

If the defendant does not appear, the plaintiff may ask for a "default" judgment. This means that if the judge decides the plaintiff has a good claim, the plaintiff can obtain a judgment without a trial because the defendant did not appear to challenge the claim.

When you go to court for the trial, take with you all the evidence you believe proves your claim. This might include a sales receipt, guarantee, lease, contract, letter or affidavit from a witness, or accident report. If a damaged article is too big to bring with you, photographs can be presented as evidence. Any witnesses you ask to speak on your behalf may write a letter or sign an affidavit, but it is best if they appear in court as well. See general information about hearings for directions on getting witnesses to appear.

Remember, a small claims case will be heard by a district court judge or district court attorney magistrate; you have no right to a jury trial, and the trial will not be recorded.

Removal from Small Claims

Either party has the right to ask that the case be heard in the general civil division of the district court. If you want to have the case moved to the general civil division of the district court, you can complete the Demand and Order for Removal, Small Claims (form DC 86), print it, and bring it to the court before or on the day of the trial. You must file the form with the court clerk. The court will notify the person filing the lawsuit if the defendant makes such a request.

In the general civil division of the district court, both the plaintiff and the defendant have the right to be represented by an attorney. Either party may also request a removal from the small claims division orally at the trial, without the need for a writing. See MCL 600.8408.

Attending the Trial

The trial will usually take place at the court where the claim was filed. It is important to be there on time; if you filed the lawsuit and are not in court when your case is called, the case will probably be dismissed. If you are the defendant and are not in court when your case is called, a default judgment may be entered against you. Bring all your relevant papers or other evidence and make sure your witnesses arrive on time.

The court clerk will call the case and both parties will appear before the district court judge or district court attorney magistrate. The judge or magistrate will ask the plaintiff to state his or her claim. When the plaintiff has finished, the defendant will have an opportunity to explain his or her side of the case. Each party should listen carefully. If either party thinks someone is leaving something out or is misstating facts, the party should be sure to tell the judge or magistrate. Both parties should take their time and tell what happened in their own words and why they think the judge or magistrate should order what they seek.

The plaintiff will be seeking the relief requested in the claim, while the defendant may ask the court to grant the relief requested, grant some other form of relief, or dismiss the claim altogether. Each party may present evidence to support his or her argument. Witnesses will be allowed to tell the court about facts that support this evidence. See general information about hearings. See also MCR 4.304 for details.

A judge's decision in the small claims division is final. Neither party can appeal to a higher court once the judge has made a decision in the small claims division. If the case is decided by a district court attorney magistrate, the case will be rescheduled before a district court judge and both parties will explain their case again.

Judgment of the Court

The court will prepare the Judgment, Small Claims (form DC 85), after the trial. The court will also make sure that the judgment is given or sent to both parties. See also MCR 4.305 and MCL 600.8410.

Collecting a Money Judgment

If you obtain a judgment against the defendant, the court will provide you with instructions regarding post-judgment collections. See the link, Collecting Money from a Judgment, available in http://courts.mi.gov. The defendant may pay the judgment plus court costs immediately after the trial, but if he/she does not have the money to pay right away, the judge may allow a reasonable time to pay and may set up a payment schedule.

If the party owing the judgment fails to pay the judgment when ordered, you must go back to the court and file additional papers to collect on the judgment by having the wages or a bank account garnished or property seized. This cannot occur until 21 days after the judgment is entered. As part of the judgment, the party owing the judgment must provide information to the court and the other party for use in post-judgment collection efforts if the judgment is not paid within 30 days. See MCR 4.305, MCL 600.8409, and MCL 600.8410.

Settlement, alternative dispute resolution, or mediation are alternatives to filing a case. Many cases are settled even when attorneys are involved. If you settle, you can work out your own result with the other person instead of having a district court judge or district court attorney magistrate do it. Many courts are offering mediation as an alternative to filing a small claims case. You may want to contact the small claims clerk to see if a mediation program is available in your community.

Appendix 6 – Illinois Eviction Process

This guide is for informational purposes only and should not be relied on for legal advice. If you need legal advice, contact an attorney.

This guide presents an overview of rules and procedures for the eviction process. The specific rules and procedures in your court may vary from those presented here. Check with your court about local rules.

How Does the Eviction Process Start?

1. The State of Illinois has a 5 Step Eviction Process:
2. Sending the Tenant a "Notice of Eviction"
3. Filing a Complaint
4. The Sheriff serves the Summons on the Tenant
5. Going to Court
6. The Sheriff removes the Tenant (if necessary)

Notice of Eviction

The first step in evicting a Tenant in Illinois is delivering the "Notice of Eviction." Depending on why you are evicting the tenant, Illinois has 3 different notice periods:

1. Five Day Notice of Eviction
   The Five Day notice is only used for non-payment of rent. It gives the Tenant 5 days to pay the rent and late fees, or Vacate the premises.
2. Ten Day Notice of Eviction
   The Ten Day Notice is used if the landlord needs to evict the tenant for violating the terms of the lease, such as unauthorized pets, illegal activity, etc. although it may also be used for non-payment of rent. Generally in Illinois, the Tenant does not have the right to cure the lease violation and stay in the property. However, in the City of Chicago and some other areas, the Tenant may have a right to cure the violation and stay.
3. Thirty Day Notice
   If the Tenant is on a month-to-month lease or an oral lease, the landlord can terminate the lease for any or no reason by simply giving a 30 Day Notice. If the tenant does not leave after 30 days, the landlord must file a Complaint to move forward with Eviction.

The notice may be delivered in the following ways:

- Personally handing the Notice to the Tenant
- Giving the Notice to someone who is at least 13 years old and who is at the Tenant's home
- Mail the Notice by Certified Mail with a Return Receipt from the Tenant
- Leaving the Notice on the Ground in front of the Tenant if they refuse to accept it
- Posting the Notice of the door of the premises if nobody is living there

If the last day of a notice period is on a weekend or holiday, then the notice period expires on the next business day. If the notice was delivered by mail, then the notice period begins when the Tenant actually receives the notice.

Affidavit of Service is a document the Landlord must sign in front of a notary, by which the landlord is swearing that he properly delivered or "served" the Tenant. This form is included with the Illinois Eviction Notice at http://www.evictionresources.com/eviction_process_articles/illinois_eviction_process.html , and will be necessary if you have to file a Complaint against a Tenant for Eviction.

Filing the Complaint

If after receiving the Notice of Eviction the Tenant has not paid the rent or cured the lease violation (if they have that option), then the landlord must sue the Tenant for eviction by filing a Complaint with the County Clerk's Office in the County where the property sits. The County Clerk's Office will have an Eviction Complaint and Summons for the Landlord to fill out and file. There will be a filing fee when the landlord files this. The Clerk will then give the Landlord a copy of the Summons and

Complaint for him to take to the Sheriff's Office to be delivered to the Tenant.

The Summons

The Summons is what the Sheriff Delivers to the Tenant telling them that they have been sued for Eviction. When the Landlord files the Complaint, the County Clerk will instruct the landlord to take a copy of the Complaint and Summons to the Sheriff's office, usually located nearby. The Sheriff will then deliver the Summons to the Tenant.

Your Day in Court

When the Landlord files the Complaint, the Clerk will give him a court date. The Landlord must show up for this court date. The landlord must take to court a copy of the Notice of Eviction, the Affidavit of Service, the Complaint, the Summons, and any witnesses or evidence needed to win the case. The landlord must tell the judge why he is entitled to possession of the property and why the Tenant should be evicted (non-payment of rent, etc.). If the Tenant does not show up, it is likely that the landlord will win by default, and the judge will grant the Landlord an Order for Eviction. If the Tenant does show up, the judge will rule after hearing both sides. After winning an Order for Eviction, the judge usually gives the Tenant 14-21 days to move.

Sheriff Removal

If a Tenant still has not moved after the fixed time ordered by the court in the Order for Eviction, the Landlord must go to the Sheriff. The Sheriff might require a deposit or fee, but will ultimately carry out the Order for Eviction and physically remove the Tenant.

All evictions in Illinois must begin with a "Notice to Leave Premises," (commonly referred to as a three-day (3-day) notice).

Note that some notices may contain extra language if you live in housing built and/or subsidized by the government.

Appendix 7 – Illinois Small Claims Process

This guide is for informational purposes only and should not be relied on for legal advice. If you need legal advice, contact an attorney.

This guide presents an overview of rules and procedures for small claims court. The specific rules and procedures in your court may vary from those presented here. Check with your court about local rules.

Introduction

Does someone owe you money? Has your landlord failed to return your security deposit even though you did not damage the rental property? Did you pay for merchandise, but the store never delivered it and won't give you a refund? You may want to consider bringing a lawsuit in small claims court. You may not need a lawyer and the rules are simpler than in most court proceedings.

Small claims court is under the jurisdiction of the Clerks of Courts Act (705 ILCS 105) and Supreme Court Rule 282. Fees are based on the population of the county and designated by county boards.

Who May Sue?

Any individual or corporation doing business in Illinois can sue or be sued in small claims court. The court may require the appointment of a guardian for those under 18 years of age.

What Types Of Cases Are Handled In Small Claims Court?

Small claims court may be used only for certain types of cases. For example:

Lawsuits such as breach of contract, property damage, or personal injury.

All evictions, regardless of the amount of rent claimed.

Repossessions of property if the property consists of consumer goods which are leased or purchased on credit from a dealer, or if the value of the property does not exceed the amount that is determined by county where filed.

Garnishments to enforce judgments from funds owed to debtors.

The maximum judgment allowed in small claims court is $10,000.00 plus costs; therefore, your claim may not exceed $10,000.00.

Is an Attorney Required?

In small claims court you can handle your personal or business legal matters without an attorney; however, you can hire an attorney to represent you if you wish. If the other party has an attorney, your chances of winning might be better if you also have an attorney.

If you do not have a lawyer and want help finding one, contact the Illinois State Bar Association's Illinois Lawyer Finder by calling (217) 525-5297or visit their website at www.IllinoisLawyerFinder.com. This service can provide you with the name of a lawyer in your area who has experience in dealing with your type of legal situation and will provide an initial consultation for an hourly fee. You do not have to hire the lawyer after the initial consultation. If you do decide to hire a lawyer to represent you in a small claims court action, be sure to ask in advance about the lawyer's fees.

Completing the Forms – Eight Step Process

1. Go to the courthouse. The small claims court clerk will supply you with the necessary forms (a summons and a complaint form) to begin the lawsuit.
2. List your name as the plaintiff. You are the person filing the lawsuit.
3. The party you are suing is called the defendant. Make sure you have the correct name and address of the defendant. If the papers can't be delivered to the defendant, you might have to start over and pay additional fees.
4. List the amount of money you request as damages.

5. Include a brief explanation about why you are suing the defendant.
6. The clerk will assign a number to each small claim case. Write down the number and refer to it in all dealings with the clerk and sheriff.
7. If you should change your address after you file your case or your appearance, be certain to notify the clerk and the opposing party of your new address. This applies if you change your phone number as well.
8. All small claims court sessions are open to the public. You may attend any of these courtroom proceedings to familiarize yourself with the procedures.

After completing the forms, they must be filed with the court. You will be charged a filing fee which differs from county to county. The filing fee must be paid in advance. Copies of the forms must then be "served on" or delivered to the defendant. Many counties allow service by regular or certified mail if the defendant lives in that county. The court will mail the forms for you, but will require a fee for this service.

Preparing Your Case

- In preparing your case, keep in mind that your proof must be more convincing than the other side's evidence. Consider the following:
- Think about how you are going to prove the defendant owes you money. Start by making a detailed list of what happened so that the facts are clear in your mind.
- Gather all written information and paperwork that pertains to the situation--contracts, rental agreements, receipts, order forms, warranties, cancelled checks, or credit card statements.
- Talk to people who may have witnessed important aspects of the dispute. For example, if you are suing your landlord for the return of your security deposit, ask

a neutral person to testify concerning the condition of the rental unit when you started renting and when you left.
- If you are suing on the basis of defective merchandise or faulty repairs, it may be very helpful to have an expert witness testify on your behalf. You might present a notarized written statement from an expert concerning the nature of the defect and the decrease in value due to the defect. However, if it becomes necessary to go to trial, you'll have to get the witness to testify in person. Full-time mechanics with several years of experience qualify as experts.

Going To Court

After your claim is filed, the court will probably set a date to review the facts in your case. Many small claims court cases are settled at this time, so come prepared to argue your case. All cases are heard by a circuit court judge and will be decided by the judge if both parties cannot reach an agreement.

Collecting the Judgment

If you win the case, ask the court to include court costs and any money you spent as part of the settlement. The court can require reimbursement for such fees as: the money paid to file the action, the cost to have the summons and complaint mailed or personally served, and any attorneys' fees.

A judgment will be entered in court stating what the opposing party owes you. In many cases, the opposing party will pay the judgment immediately. In other instances, you may find it necessary to take further informal action or consult an attorney who can proceed with more formal legal steps to collect the debt. The court will not force the defendant to pay what is owed you.

The court will order the debtor to provide a disclosure statement to you or to the clerk of the court within 15 days of entry of the judgment. The statement must contain the debtor's name and address, his or her employer and the employer's address, any real property owned by the debtor, cash on hand and financial institutions in which the debtor has funds.

If you are unable to satisfy the judgment by contacting the other party, contact the clerk of the court that heard your case. From the clerk, you can obtain the forms necessary for garnishment proceedings--if the other party receives wages or has bank accounts.

Remember, there is always the possibility that the small claims court will not rule in your favor. Carefully consider all your options before proceeding with a lawsuit. If you do decide to bring a lawsuit in small claims court, prepare carefully to increase your chances of success.

Some points to remember:

- Information in this brochure is not a substitute for legal advice from an attorney.
- Court staff may not give you legal advice.
- Know the rules and procedures of your court.
- Meet all deadlines.
- Follow through on your responsibilities.
- Keep copies of all documents.
- Small claims court can only resolve claims about money.